Sex, Brains, and Video Games

ALA Editions purchases fund advocacy, awareness, and accreditation programs for library professionals worldwide.

Sex, Brains, and Video Games

Information and Inspiration
for Youth Services Librarians

SECOND EDITION

JENNIFER BUREK PIERCE

An imprint of the American
Library Association

Chicago   2017

Jennifer Burek Pierce is associate professor in the School of Library & Information Science at the University of Iowa. Books, games, and toys for young people are of particular interest to her, as is the marketing of these materials. Her books include *What Adolescents Ought to Know: Sexual Health Texts in Early 20th Century America* (UMass Press, 2011) and *Sex, Brains, and Video Games: A Librarian's Guide to Teens in the Twenty-First Century* (ALA Editions, 2008). She developed the Youth Matters column for *American Libraries* and has also written for *The Chronicle of Higher Education*. She serves on the advisory board for the Iowa Initiative for Sustainable Communities, the University of Iowa's center for community engagement.

ISBNs
978-0-8389-1548-6 (paper)
978-0-8389-1549-3 (PDF)
978-0-8389-1550-9 (ePub)
978-0-8389-1551-6 (Kindle)

Library of Congress Cataloging-in-Publication Data
Names: Burek Pierce, Jennifer, author.
Title: Sex, brains, and video games : information and inspiration for youth services
    librarians / Jennifer Burek Pierce.
Description: Second edition. | Chicago : ALA Editions, an imprint of the American
    Library Association, 2017. | Includes bibliographical references and index.
Identifiers: LCCN 2017001197 | ISBN 9780838915486 (pbk. : alk. paper) | ISBN
    9780838915493 (pdf) | ISBN 9780838915509 (epub) | ISBN 9780838915516
    (kindle)
Subjects: LCSH: Libraries and teenagers—United States. | Young adults' libraries—
    United States. | Adolescence—United States. | Teenagers—United States.
Classification: LCC Z718.5.B87 2017 | DDC 027.62/6—dc23 LC record available
    at https://lccn.loc.gov/2017001197

Cover design by Alejandra Diaz. Images © Adobe Stock. Text design and composition by Dianne M. Rooney in Sabon and Univers typefaces.

♾ This paper meets the requirements of ANSI/NISO Z39.48–1992 (Permanence of Paper).

Printed in the United States of America

21 20 19 18 17   5 4 3 2 1

For MRB and HS

Contents

Acknowledgments

Numerous individuals supported the first edition of *Sex, Brains, and Video Games*, which was my first book. Among them were professor emerita Mary K. Chelton, former *American Libraries* editor and publisher Leonard Kniffel, retired AL senior editor Beverly Goldberg, and Bethany Templeton Klem, now head of children's services at the Bedford Free Public Library in Massachusetts. Michael Bonin was responsible for my introduction to Jay Giedd's theories, the lynchpin of this work, and more, and Herb Snyder read pages and pages of prose in the process of its completion. The new edition was no less involved, and multiple people were instrumental to its completion. They include Mary Smith of the Mount Prospect Public Library in Illinois, who invited me to speak about the themes of this book for LACONI. University of Iowa graduate assistant Andy Petersen helped to compile the research that supported the presentation, and Kery Lawson's work formatting and reading chapters during the revision process was a tremendous asset. Colleagues Rachel Black, Chelsee

Bumann, Kara Logsden, Kate McDowell, Lindsay Mattock, Beth Paul, and Cindy Welch read sections of the manuscript in progress, and I appreciate their willingness to preview and comment on my work. ALA Editions editor Jamie Santoro has been a warm, patient, and gracious guide along the way to this new edition. Without these individuals and ALA Editions' editors and staff, then and now, this project would have been inconceivable. My debts, and my gratitude, are deep.

Introduction

The first edition of this book began ten years ago. Following an Urban Libraries Council conference in Chicago, where I learned about innovative work on adolescence in cognitive science and sociology, I began to refer to those theories of development in my popular and scholarly writing. These articles were regarded as the first ones in library and information science (LIS) to acknowledge the work of pioneering researchers like Jay Giedd, whose findings reshaped paradigms used to explain the maturation processes that play out during the teen years. As interest in that emerging brain research grew, I was asked to write the book that became *Sex, Brains, and Video Games: A Librarian's Guide to Teens in the Twenty-First Century,* and ten years later, evolving research and other developments prompt its revision. Key concepts, including the history of young adult services and the nature of research on adolescence and U.S. adolescents, preface a fuller explanation of prevailing themes in our encounters with teens.

Although much has happened since the first decade of the twenty-first century, I have the good fortune to remain the audience for the stories of students and graduates who work in youth services. Despite laments for those whose passion for working with teens has been confounded by combative library administrations, others acknowledge myriad difficulties and even bad days before rushing forward to realize their visions and plans. They tell me about their strategies for ensuring teens whose financial circumstances might jeopardize their access to library resources can use computers and collaborate—or even just socialize—with friends in teen spaces. They renew their collection management strategies to ensure teens can find graphic novels and pursue new possibilities in makerspaces. They propose programs that facilitate teens' abilities to communicate directly with community leaders. They share information in conversations with teens, even if there is a poster with that same information on a wall three feet behind them. They know whatever they do, they will need to revisit their assumptions, make new connections, and renew their efforts with each new cohort of young people. These librarians, so full of commitment and energy, are awesome and inspiring. They are also, according to one historical interpretation of the field, positioned at the beginning of the second century of young adult library services in this country.[1]

Meanwhile, the research that was beginning to offer distinctive conclusions about adolescence has gained explanatory power and depth. Where there was much curiosity about better understanding the teen brain, these days one can find defensive, even angry, critiques of the empirical research that has sought to better understand how teens change during puberty and adolescence. Then, we had a handful of articles that encouraged awareness of the complexities of gender identity, and now we witness both significant advances in LGBTQ rights and adamant political opposition. Many dynamics, whether the result of research, technology, or social change, encourage a new look at contemporary adolescence.

At the opening of the 2016 Public Library Association conference, Sari Feldman observed that libraries "are a lifeline for people at every key transition in their lives."[2] Adolescence represents one of these critical times in a life, a transition with much importance and potential. While some advocates for teens have argued that LIS should create its own concept of this stage rather than relying on extant models of adolescent development, there are multiple realities in play.[3] One is that teens are minors, not yet adults, in the U.S. legal system that governs their rights. Regardless of librarians' respect, teens may be subject to municipal curfews and other restrictions or oversight, and these laws factor into their relationships with the library. In most states, their education is compulsory, rather than voluntary, well into the teen years; Arizona, Vermont, and Wyoming allow students to leave school soonest, once pupils reach age sixteen or complete tenth grade.[4] Their legal status also affects their relationships with their parents or guardians, despite whatever privacy library policies afford their reference questions and circulation transactions. Declarations that some teens are more mature than 30-year-olds, however true in individual cases, matter little in these contexts.[5] Further, the number of studies showing that teens with strong support from their families fare better both during adolescence and after is increasing. Many conditions suggest the value of a shared understanding of what it means to be an adolescent, considered broadly rather than from a narrow, discipline-specific construct.

One reason to think about what researchers in cognate fields know about teens lies in our own field's renewed attention to community engagement and partnerships. As we work with others to make teens welcome in our libraries and connected to our communities, interdisciplinary knowledge, specifically a thorough, contemporary understanding of adolescence supported by research from fields like education, sociology, and communication, should guide our approach to this time of change in a young person's life. This book supports librarians' efforts to gain familiarity with those ideas.

THE PURPOSE OF YOUNG ADULT SERVICES, THEN AND NOW

When we provide library services to young adults, we aspire to two fundamental objectives: to engage adolescents through meaningful and appealing responses to their recreational and informational needs, and to support good outcomes for young people as their roles change. This dual purpose creates a balancing act for library professionals as we try to figure out what teens want while making what they need available too, not unlike the complications of welcoming them into library spaces while preserving a level of decorum that allows other patrons their own uses of the library. These aims may appear straightforward, reflecting a commonsense approach to serving young people, and many advocates of youth services have long espoused them. Think of Samuel S. Green's description of youth services when he wrote in 1879, "I would also have in every library a friend of the young, whom they can consult freely when in want of assistance, and who, in addition to the power of gaining their confidence, has knowledge and tact enough to render them real aid in making selections."[6] Mary K. Chelton has observed that in 1917 the New York Public Library (NYPL) hired a librarian to respond to the needs of young people "who were aging out of children's services, but who were often not yet well-served by the library's adult services units."[7] These are two instances of the profession's openness to teens, signals that despite the all-too-easy-to-find historical statements that disparaged adolescents, some leaders looked for a way to respond to young adults' distinctive needs. What it means, on the one hand, to make the library a welcoming environment for teens, while on the other, to help them assume adult roles, has varied considerably over time. A quick glance at the profession's past offers examples of librarians' ideas about youth services that contrast starkly with our own, as well as similarities to our present ideals.

We can find evidence that in the earliest years of the profession, librarians were concerned that their young patrons read too much and wanted the wrong sorts of books. Their views, distinctive for critiques that seem unbelievable now, represented one perspective on library services to teens. The 1879 complaints of librarian Mary A. Bean against young people's "craze for books" and "indiscriminate reading" were as laudable to her contemporaries as they are laughable to us.[8] Bean's concerns, though, were very much congruent with the thinking of her time, which represented the early years of both librarianship and psychology. To Bean and other professionals, adolescents were sometimes trying but not unsympathetic individuals who could be encouraged to give up romances or adventure stories, moving from questionable books to an appreciation of the classics that showed real discernment. According to this school of thought, teens were unformed but educable, barring the influence of the wrong sorts of peers, whether in person or on the page.

There were serious concerns that frivolous or racy books would derail young people's futures in this life and damn them in the next. In 1895, George Cole warned librarians that

> nowadays a child who can read will read; and if we do not lead and direct his taste, the enemy, who is ever lying in wait for poor, faltering humanity, will give the child abundant opportunity of the knowledge of evil; and this evil, whose knowledge is death to the soul of every pure boy or girl, is crowding us at every corner of life.[9]

These pronouncements encouraged late nineteenth-century librarians working with young people to bear a rather weighty responsibility for their patrons' futures. Teens were regarded as poor judges of their own recreational reading matter, and librarians became their protectors against books that hinted at real-world dangers. Librarians strove to shape young minds in preparation for adult lives and careers, much as their contemporaries in Progressive Era reform intended to improve society. When the first full-length book on adolescent psychology appeared in the early twentieth century, the author of *Adolescence* became a prominent speaker at library and education conferences, cautioning librarians and teachers about the harm that could result from young people's reading habits. Although he also urged adults to remember their own adolescent years and empathize with teens, writers today tend to focus on his dramatic pronouncements about what could go wrong during the teen years.

Amid these fears, there were hints of change. Although librarians lacked the professional nomenclature that now distinguishes teens from children, there was discussion of how the needs of adolescents differed from the very young. At the same time that many librarians writing for the early *Library Journal,* which was then the name of

ALA's magazine, objected vociferously to books with stories that depicted lives and actions that seemed improbable—a teen's ability to take charge of a runaway train or a romance that promised luxury instead of hard work—others did not. Historians examining actual library records from this era have found something surprising in light of these well-publicized complaints about teens' reading habits. While it seems likely that many librarians did censor their collections, several recent historical studies reveal ample evidence that contested authors like Horatio Alger, Oliver Optic, and others were part of libraries' collections.[10] In other words, as some librarians loudly condemned certain authors as inappropriate, others quietly circulated what people, including adolescents, wanted to read.

Our belief in the value of leisure reading, freely chosen, has these and other historical antecedents. Teens' rights to access a wide range of materials are declared in documents as old as the 1953 Freedom to Read Statement and, more recently, ALA opposition to legislation like the Deleting Online Predators Act of 2006 (H.R. 5319, 109th Cong.) and subsequent efforts to limit access to online content. Declarations that young people as well as adults have the right to read and view a wide range of materials, according to their interests rather than their ages, are mirrored in another proclamation of readers' rights that includes the "right to skip pages" and the "right not to finish."[11] A plethora of policy statements commit us to collections that serve young people in meaningful, expansive ways, and we are joined in this endeavor by peer professional organizations and individuals, like the Office for Intellectual Freedom, the National Council of Teachers of English, and authors from Judy Blume to John Green, who support librarians and educators facing materials challenges.[12] We've shifted over the years from emphatic statements about the imperative of safeguarding teens to ensuring their access to a brave new world of information and entertainment resources, with respect for the young person's growing autonomy as she creates an independent and newly adult identity.

The professional literature in our journals and magazines extends this theme in other directions. There are expressions of concern about incursions against young people's rights to privacy: Should parents be able to review library records to see what books their child has borrowed? Does this change when fines or replacement fees are incurred? Can parents limit the materials to which their child has access, whether this involves books parents disapprove of or R-rated DVDs? Is it a violation of professional ethics to allow parents, as at least a few libraries quietly do, to request special library cards that restrict their children to checking out material from the children's collection? Should parents or guardians be involved in reference transactions? Many writers have argued that young people's rights merit absolute defense. There is research that evokes a compelling image of young people as independent, perhaps even abandoned by their traditional caregivers; lacking safe places and well-intentioned advisors; without resources, dependent on our sympathy and our resources.[13] It's more than a truism to say we've come a long way since the first years of the profession in this country; it is indisputably true.

Philosopher and poet George Santayana famously observed in his *Life of Reason,* "Those who cannot remember the past are condemned to repeat it." In librarianship, we credit ourselves with remembering information history—times when people were denied access to materials thought to be sensitive or controversial and times when people were prohibited from using libraries because of their age, their national origin, their politics, or the color of their skin. In an effort not to repeat those dark times, we have articulated goals of providing services to all, including young people.

Yet this enthusiasm can overshadow other elements of the profession's past—chiefly, awareness of the relevant expertise of other fields. Some have argued that, when psychologist G. Stanley Hall published his two-volume work *Adolescence* in 1909, he invented both adolescence and adolescent psychology.[14] Librarians were among those who considered his advice as they grappled with efforts to serve and guide the young people who entered their facilities. As the twentieth century wore on, efforts to understand teens persisted. A writer for *Publishers Weekly* in 1929 observed, "Of recent years the adolescent girl has been much in the public eye. Her psychology, her behavior problems, her needs, all have been discussed at great length."[15] Librarians followed these discussions. The American discovery of adolescence and the reform impulses of the Progressive Era informed librarians' interests in young people.

Many ideas about youth services put forth by Progressive Era librarians, among whom Bean and Cole could be numbered, would strike few of us as truly progressive. Yet as the Progressive Era unfolded, these librarians did something right in seeking out the ideas and advice of those whose research in the social and behavioral sciences would contribute to their ability to work effectively with young people. They believed their own professional training could and should be supplemented by other kinds of information about teens. They found that their work with adolescents would be improved by seeking out ideas beyond the boundaries of their own field. Educators and psychologists were among the experts these professionals consulted, and librarians monitored prominent general-readership magazines that published commentaries about young people and books.

It has been argued that providing library services in a dynamic contemporary environment is most appropriately guided by the profession's core values and enduring principles. I argue that professional service to young adults requires librarians to have an informed understanding of adolescence as well as strong beliefs in service and access. More than personal memories, however deeply felt, of that sometimes strange and awkward time, librarians' sense of what it means to be an adolescent should derive from contemporary research that offers changing and even challenging perspectives about our young clientele. More than knowledge of current young adult titles, the latest teen enthusiasms, or even the LIS research literature should inform a young adult librarian's professional practice. The work of other disciplines can help us as we think about the issues involved in balancing our efforts to connect with teens and to support their transition into adult life; it can also help us as we communicate with other professionals invested in teens' success, safety, and happiness.

Who Is a Young Adult?

At an ALA Conference panel for young adult librarians, one practitioner asked, "Who is the young adult?" The problem, she observed, was that different people seemed to describe entirely different age groups when using the phrase librarians have adopted for patrons between the ages of twelve and eighteen. How were young adult librarians to know when someone talking about young adults was actually talking about young adults? This librarian was correct in noticing that the people who are called young adults don't always belong to the group she intends to serve; further, the clientele of young adult departments may be given different names as well.

Those outside LIS who work with young people have different vocabularies that reflect the history and norms of their respective fields. Many other disciplines, including public health and psychology, refer to the group we call young adults as *adolescents.* Adolescence has been divided into three phases—early, middle, and late—to acknowledge the developmental and cultural differences between the experiences of a thirteen-year-old and an eighteen-year-old.[16] Still, there may be instances when other fields use our preferred term or the cohort that an author describes includes teens as well as slightly older individuals. The surest assumption when someone outside the profession uses *young adults* to describe a group is that this person refers to individuals who are no longer of middle school or high school age. To these and other researchers, young adults are eighteen and older—in other words, those who have recently gained legal status as adults in the United States. The combined newness of their status as adults and their age relative to others in the cohort makes them young adults.

Librarians' choice of the term *young adults* came about in 1957 after years of using a variety of terms to talk about teens. The early journal literature of the field discusses services for "intermediates" and "older boys and girls." Despite the contention that the term *teenager* came about as the result of marketing and advertising campaigns following World War II, variations on that phrase were in use as these early professionals sought to work with teens.[17] One occurrence was a 1919 sex education pamphlet that spoke directly to its audience of *teens*.[18] Margaret Edwards, a key figure in the development of modern young adult services, disliked the word. One can hear both the lingering newness of the expression and Edwards's disdain for it. Like Dennett, she used scare quotes around the term when she wrote, "'Teen-agers,' besides being a bit undignified, may sound patronizing or scornful and does not seem to include the more mature sixteen- to nineteen-year-olds." She seemed resigned to the inadequacy of the profession's label for her young clientele: "Who are young adults? They are people in their teens for whom there is no adequate nomenclature."[19] Nonetheless, the label has endured, and in recent years its meaning seems to be on the verge of changing, as *tweens*, or preteens, have become a market for young adult books. Some librarians have offered tween programs for children as young as eight, despite its original reference to the ages of ten to twelve, the numeric cusp of the teen years.

Tweens, despite its rhyming resonance with the word *teens*, is not necessarily in widespread use. When I've used the expression in a class for undergraduates, their puzzlement and disbelief was evident; it's not a label that young people have claimed as their own. I was struck by the awkwardness of a teacher's flailing attempts to find a collective noun for her sixth-grade students in Richard Peck's *The Best Man*. Peck captures adolescents' not unkind disdain as adolescent narrator Archer Magill notes his teacher's "rookie mistakes" in this regard. When new student teacher and reservist Mr. McLeod greets the class, "Good afternoon, troops," Archer is ecstatic. "Troops!" he exclaims to himself. "That's all we called ourselves from then on. It was way better than boys and people."[20] ■

PROFESSIONS INVESTED IN ADOLESCENCE
Information Sources and Potential Partners

Who else is interested in teens and their developmental outcomes? What information do they have that can help us help teens? Educators have long been seen as librarians' partners, given our shared investment in young people's literacy. Researchers in several other disciplines want to know more about young adults as media consumers, computer users, health-care recipients, and simply as growing and changing individuals. These fields are identified and described briefly to provide an overview of prevailing research methods, and information sources are included that may be useful to librarians. Practitioners in these fields may be potential partners for librarians who are involved in outreach and other programming for young adults.

Communication researchers are strongly interested in teens' involvement with mass media. Their definition of *mass media* encompasses television and radio, magazines and newspapers, the World Wide Web and blogs, video games, movies, and music. These researchers use diverse methods to see what programs and pages attract teen attention, what teens make of the media, and what effects media consumption has on teens. The processes by which media create their effects are also of interest. Consequently, communication researchers examine trends in teens' media use and what they make of the information available through all sorts of communication channels.

Some communication researchers focus on interpersonal communication—the interactions that occur between two people or small clusters of individuals. These researchers attend to patterns of expression and barriers to effective communication, including intergenerational conversation and related issues.

Health researchers may be in schools of medicine or public health, in departments of nursing or specialty fields. There are also federal, state, and municipal health departments that collect data and carry out programs to assess and protect the public's well-being. Collectively, these researchers and practitioners produce a simply astounding body of literature each year. Among the massive number of publications are articles concerned with teens' healthy development. Some of these materials address basic health-care matters such as access to doctors and clinics, while others focus on reproductive health and risk-taking behaviors that may distinguish teens from children. Based on behavioral assessments, surveys, and other research, these studies identify the kinds of health information that young people need and also consider teens' information-gathering practices. The result is a rich body of literature that can enhance librarians' efforts to offer teens meaningful and accurate nonfiction materials.

Ever since G. Stanley Hall argued that adolescents were a distinctive population subject to emotional and intellectual turbulence while maturation processes played out, psychologists have been interested in teenagers. In the twenty-first century, researchers in adolescent psychology have considerably more tools at their disposal than the field's pioneers did at the start of the twentieth century. Neuropsychology, a specialized research area, examines "the relation between brain and human cognitive, emotional, and behavioral function."[21] Some neuropsychologists use magnetic resonance imaging (MRI) and other new technology to capture brain images that provide insights into activity and change at different ages. Other studies also contribute to a changing understanding of adolescence. Because much of this research is still new, researchers sometimes report observations that contradict previous thinking but are not yet able to provide specific recommendations that might guide our interactions with teens. Nonetheless, recent and ongoing work in psychology replaces the theories of Piaget and other developmental psychologists whose models once explained youth development, relegating them to figures in the history of youth development, rather than current theorists.

Education research, like the research undertaken in psychology, employs a range of methods and comprises numerous special areas. Some work includes scrutiny of newer genres, like graphic novels, as means of encouraging reluctant readers. Other researchers are considering how the dynamics of video games translate into learning. Their findings regarding literacy and learning are of potential use for librarians.

These are some of the fields from which LIS practitioners can draw in their efforts to provide meaningful and appropriate services to young adults. Studies conducted in these areas alternately build on and revise what we know about young people. Given the nature of the revisions that are suggested by this research, though, understanding what is taking place outside the profession is increasingly important as we collaborate with others invested in ensuring the well-being and healthy development of the teens who visit our libraries.

~~~~~~

Reading the Research Guidance and Questions

Ideas about adolescent development are presented in numerous outlets, including interdisciplinary research literature. One way of thinking about research is to see it as an extended, asynchronous conversation with a dispersed set of peers and colleagues. Even if you are the lone teen services librarian in your community, there are others with your passions and problems. When they put forward their ideas, whether in print or podcasts, you have the opportunity to join a dialogue about your shared expertise. The possibilities of e-mail and Twitter make it possible to reach out to these writers, to share your responses. What follows are my suggestions about how you might approach the ranging sources of perspective on adolescence, literature, and librarianship that are available to us today.

Research literature, whether developed by faculty or practitioners, serves many ends in libraries. It allows us to learn about innovation taking place elsewhere, thus aiding the implementation of our initiatives. It alerts us to new uses of technology, shifting trends, and revisions of historically accepted facts that might ask us to modify our services. That said, just as other fields have their own ways of talking about teens, they will have different means of conducting research. There are multiple, valid approaches to research problems, so interdisciplinary scholarly work reflects a range of evidentiary bases and conclusions. As librarians consider the claims about teens put forward in venues from the evening news to scholarly journals, understanding categories of scholarly work and professional writing facilitates our evaluation of the proliferation of publications about young people.

Further, an increasing demand that libraries and other professional, nonprofit entities demonstrate *outcomes,* or the effects of their services, means young adult librarians need to participate in larger discussions about how we know libraries matter. Reading research literature can help us make the case for services and resources when it articulates successes in similar situations. Research can model strategies for reporting outcomes, conserving the time we have for outreach and other important, community-based activities.

Even more theoretical work has value. One of my professors used to recite this explanatory mantra to us, and now I say this to my students: "The role of theory is to predict, to describe, or to explain." What changes in services or resources would you anticipate as the result of reading about teens today? What descriptions of adolescence and others' support for teens' futures spur new thinking in your community? How might you explain changes, like decreased program attendance or increased circulation? Used strategically, familiarity with research is more than another demand on a librarian's time; it helps us think through the myriad decisions inherent in professional life.

Reflecting on the diverse sources of information and ideas that contextualize and educate librarians should be a regular part of professional life. This overview of research characteristics incorporates questions that can guide evaluation of the literature, whether produced in LIS or a field whose terminology, at first glance, is baffling.

A *literature review* is a key part of most scholarly work. Often, a literature review introduces and grounds a study or an experiment; sometimes, however, a literature review may be an independent undertaking with the sole purpose of analyzing or synthesizing extant research. In the latter case, the researcher may be interested in the ways different disciplines regard a common interest, in evidence of disparate understandings despite presumed common ground, or in the way a field's understanding has changed over time. (In essence, this book is a literature review that brings multiple aspects of contemporary research on adolescents into conversation for the benefit of librarians.) In either case, a literature review highlights what is known and draws attention to limitations or gaps that warrant further attention.

- If you are reading a literature review, consider

  What dates and disciplines does the study cover? Is its emphasis on recency and disciplinarity, or does it aim to be comprehensive?

What questions does it raise? Does the author suggest a path for responding to those questions?

Does it describe, telling you what others have said, or is it analytical, drawing conclusions and offering insights as a result of its compilations?

The distinction between *basic* and *applied research* reflects the nature of the argument put forward in a research project: is its aim to establish knowledge, or is the aim to solve a particular problem in the field? *Basic research,* the agenda of many studies that document the nature of cognitive change and growth in the brain during adolescence, is focused on establishing what can be known. Technologies that create new research techniques are among the factors that encourage researchers to revisit fundamental assumptions. It may be a precursor to research that solves problems, but a major role of basic research is to advance theory and support further study. A related, newer concept is *translational research,* which looks for ways to bring more conceptual research to bear on practice. Although it has been argued that the difference between basic and *applied research* is a continuum, rather than a polarity, applied research usually addresses questions related to practice and real-world scenarios.[22]

- If you are reading basic research, can you discern the theory or theories under consideration?

   the problem or issue in knowledge that is being reviewed?

   whether knowledge is confirmed or modified as a result of the study? (Are the results the basis for a new hypothesis, preliminary, or more definitive?)

- If you are reading a more applied form of research, does the study

   indicate what problem or problems are being addressed and why?

   offer solutions or directions for change? (Are these possibilities institutional or more broadly applicable?)

Another common, if not always neat, distinction is between *quantitative* and *qualitative research.* Much work in the humanities is qualitative, drawing on language and images in archival documents, films, and narratives for evidence to support a central argument. A quantitative study derives its power from numbers, which may range from simple descriptive statistics that create a portrait of a population or a place, to more complex calculations that require specialized computer programs and expert training to create inferences and claim causal relationships.

- When you consult a quantitative study, consider

  What population is being studied? How was it created? Researchers differentiate between a random sample, where all members of a defined group have an equal chance of being selected, and more purposive or convenience samples, where the population is selected for a particular reason or is simply a matter of who is willing to participate in the project. A study with a random sample or one whose sampling results in a population like your community is more likely to produce results that can effectively guide your work. A location-specific focus group, for example, does not inherently possess attributes that will hold true elsewhere.

  How was the study conducted? For decades researchers have noted problems with phone surveys since not everyone owns a phone. While few studies are impervious to critique, consider whether there are blind spots in the construction that might affect results unduly.

  Does the researcher provide the questions that participants were asked, allowing insight into her process?

- When you assess qualitative research, consider

  What is the aim and central argument? Because qualitative research does not always reflect a defined, preexisting method of analysis, a researcher should be clear about purpose.

What is offered as proof? Textual studies, biography, and several other approaches tend to quote heavily from their sources to represent their subjects. Historical work relies on footnotes that reflect the researcher's path through the primary sources found in archives. In most cases, a reader should be able to understand the material that forms the basis for the ideas under consideration.

Whose story is told through this project? Why?

What does the author want you to understand? Is this a new dimension of professional or institutional history? Is it an argument for the value of including particular types of material in a collection? Does it ask you to perceive a community in new ways?

Scholars also may see their work as either *empirical* or *critical research*. Empirical research has a long tradition of generating observation-based conclusions. Originally associated with the scientific method, its allegiance to arguments driven by data, whether quantitative or archival, makes it a touchstone for some researchers in the humanities as well. *Critical studies,* broadly speaking, are invested in using scholarly tools to scrutinize cultural norms that countenance bias or inequality. Numerous subdisciplines adopt this approach to scholarship. Work in this vein has a theoretical allegiance and an objective of social transformation.[23]

- When considering the philosophical orientation of a research project, be attuned to these sorts of issues:

    Does the author acknowledge the perspective from which he writes, either directly or indirectly? If he aligns with a theorist or a critical school, do you understand the basic tenets? What assumptions characterize the supporting work?

    What is the author's agenda?

What are you asked to know or do as the result of the ideas in this scholarly essay?

Best practices research attempts to learn from others in order to choose the most effective, appropriate course for one's own library. Best practices articles may be seen as an evolution of what were once labeled "how we done it good" articles, often belittled as lacking context or self-critique.[24] The intent of best practices literature is to identify the factors most likely to result in desirable outcomes. *Case studies,* which examine the strengths and weaknesses of a particular library endeavor to arrive at recommendations for those involved in similar projects, are a related kind of research. Where best practices articles emphasize a comparative approach to the issue under consideration, typically generated from the library literature, case studies rely more on what is known as *thick description,* an approach associated with Clifford Geertz, coined to describe the detailed work of conveying a situation or phenomenon to those at a remove from it.[25] Thick description, despite its name, supports analytical claims; analysis and evaluation are also integral to best practices articles.

- When considering the utility of articles or books in this category, you might be attuned to the following details:

  Is the work of a single library or multiple organizations evaluated? Is the guidance offered reflective of those circumstances?

  Is the report a positive overview, or does it acknowledge and suggest how to prepare for difficulties?

  What details are provided? Can you tell how many branches and staff were involved in a program? Is the number of hours or the overall time frame for preparations identified? Was financial support provided, and if so, where did it come from?

  What represents a positive outcome? Why?

There is a specialized type of scholarly writing referred to as a *think piece.* The think piece may be regarded as the product of expertise and experience, the informed expression of ideas, less the scholarly apparatus of investigation. The author of a think piece may want to raise questions about common assumptions in the field or how we should respond to current events. This kind of essay may precede further, more conventionally constructed research on the subject.

- If you are reading a think piece, you might want to know

    Is this author breaking new ground or participating in conversation with other individuals?

    Is a new concern under discussion, or might it be something that has fallen off our collective radar for a while and deserves new attention?

    Do questions of your own result from reading this author? Does the essay spark new questions for you?

Research does not eliminate risk. We still may see low turnout for events, books that don't circulate, and services that flop. Still, we can justify risk and manage some difficulties by an informed approach to our work. By considering how or why an article or book was constructed, we are better positioned to evaluate its argument and its relevance to our concerns. Since each approach to research has its own norms, we can consider whether the evidence presented is congruent with the conventions of its scholarly mode, as well as whether the conclusions presented serve our aims of understanding and serving teens. ■

UNDERSTANDING ADOLESCENCE, HERE AND NOW

There is increasing attention to youth development, and there are many efforts to follow the emerging understandings of young people, not just in academia but in the popular press as well. Magazine covers and news stories call attention to the ways that young people in the twenty-first century differ from previous generations, if not because of what these teens and tweens know and do, then because of what is known about them. There are discussions of how the brain grows and changes, whether girls' and boys' brains harbor sex-linked differences, teens' sleep patterns and alertness, and the social environments in which adolescents operate, including social-networking apps like Facebook, Snapchat, and Tumblr. It has become almost routine to hear that one app is popular with teens, only to learn that it has been abandoned in favor of some newer tool once the popularity of an app extends to older users; at the same time, it is also possible to find indicators of continued use of a supposedly dead platform. See, for example, the contention that Facebook is passé, an outlet for parents and even grandparents, versus a media commentary that documented a younger generation's disenchantment with voice mail by sharing one purportedly representative young man's comment: "I guess I usually just assume that it's probably not that important if you didn't text me, and you didn't send me a message on Facebook."[26] It seems to be acknowledged everywhere that young people form a distinct culture whether because of what happens in their heads or what they do with new media.

Librarians must attend to these conversations. The diversity of places where information about adolescence and adolescents can be found—it is no longer the province of scholarly journals that demand a technical vocabulary—has increased the accessibility of evolving ideas about adolescence. This aids our ability to develop services and programs that are in tune with teens' sense of their own needs and with experts on young people in other fields. The conclusions that can be drawn from skilled research and interpretation will change as time passes and more is learned, but the community of youth services practitioners should recognize the importance of such projects. Understanding does not mean simple acceptance; we must evaluate the conclusions that scientists and other scholars are forming so that we can determine how and when to apply their knowledge to our own work with young people. In the end, doing so may mean raising our own questions about young adults in addition to considering others' answers.

This book examines the perspectives of cognate fields that seek to understand the conditions of U.S. adolescents and can speak to our work with young adults in libraries. It invokes empirical research to explore common themes of young adulthood, like maturation, sexuality, and identity. It calls attention to research that invites us to ask questions about our assumptions about teens and our professional practices. It points toward change, but its scope does not include all elements of that change. Instead, it outlines key areas of interest, gives attention to leading scholars and their work, and recommends resources that librarians might enjoy and find informative. In all this, this book suggests ways of thinking about young adults and communicating with others who, like us, aspire to help teens as they seek meaning and fulfillment for their present and future selves.

NOTES

1. Mary K. Chelton, "Roots and Branches: YA Services Past, Present and Future: The First YALSA Past President's Lecture," presentation, Young Adult Library Services Association Midwinter Meeting, San Diego, CA, September 8, 2011, http://yalsa.ala.org/blog/wp-content/uploads/2011/01/2011_past_presidents _lecture_chelton.pdf.
2. Sari Feldman, "Libraries Transform: Opening General Session," presentation, Public Library Association 2016 Conference, Denver, CO, April 5–9, 2016.
3. Anthony Bernier, *Transforming Young Adult Services* (Chicago: ALA Neal-Schuman, 2013).
4. "Table 5.1. Compulsory school attendance laws, minimum and maximum age limits for required free education, by state: 2015," State Education Reforms, 2015, https://nces.ed.gov/programs/statereform/tab5_1.asp.
5. Mike Males, "Tribalism versus Citizenship: Are Youth Increasingly Unwelcome in Libraries?" in *Transforming Young Adult Services*, ed. Anthony Bernier, 151–70 (Chicago: ALA Neal-Schuman, 2013).
6. Samuel S. Green, "Sensational Fiction in Public Libraries," *Library Journal* 4 (1879): 345–55.
7. Chelton, "Roots and Branches."
8. Mary A. Bean, "Evil of Unlimited Freedom in the Use of Juvenile Fiction," *Library Journal* 4 (1879): 343.

9. George Watson Cole, "How Teachers Should Cooperate with Libraries," *Library Journal* 20 (1895): 115.

10. Frank Felsenstein and James J. Connolly, *What Middletown Read: Print Culture in an American Small City* (Amherst: University of Massachusetts Press, 2015); Christine Pawley, *Reading on the Middle Border: The Culture of Print in Late-Nineteenth-Century Osage, Iowa* (Amherst: University of Massachusetts Press, 2001); Jennifer Burek Pierce and Mikki Smith, "Oliver Optic and Young America: Reading Library Shelves and Publishing Records for Insights into the Past for Perspective on Technological and Cultural Change," in *Annual Review of Cultural Heritage Informatics 2015* (Lanham, MD: Rowman & Littlefield, 2016).

11. American Library Association and Association of American Publishers, *The Freedom to Read Statement,* June 30, 2004, www.ala.org/advocacy/intfreedom/statementspols/freedomreadstatement; American Film and Video Association, *Freedom to View Statement,* endorsed by the American Library Association January 10, 1990, www.ala.org/advocacy/intfreedom/statementspols/freedomviewstatement; Daniel Pennac, *The Rights of the Reader,* trans. Sarah Adams (Somerville, MA: Candlewick Press, 2008), 145; American Library Association letter opposing the *Deleting Online Predators Act of 2006,* www.ala.org/yalsa/sites/ala.org.yalsa/files/content/professionaltools/DOPAInfoPacket.pdf.

12. National Council of Teachers of English, *The Students' Right to Read,* 2013, www.ncte.org/positions/statements/righttoreadguideline.

13. Jama Shelton and Julie Winkelstein, "Safe in the Stacks: Public Libraries Serving LGBTQ Homeless Youth," presentation, Public Library Association 2016 Conference, Denver, CO, April 5–9, 2016.

14. Jeffrey Moran, *Teaching Sex: The Shaping of Adolescence in the Twentieth Century* (Cambridge, MA: Harvard University Press, 2000).

15. M. A. Ashley, "Sex O'clock in America," *Publishers' Weekly* (October 26, 1929), 2077.

16. Morris Green and Judith S. Palfrey, eds., *Bright Futures: Guidelines for Health Supervision of Infants, Children, and Adolescents,* 2nd ed. (Arlington, VA: National Center for Education in Maternal and Child Health, 2002).

17. Thomas Hine, *The Rise and Fall of the American Teenager* (New York: Avon Books, 1999).

18. Mary Ware Dennett, *The Sex Side of Life: An Explanation for Young People* (1919), http://archive.org/stream/thesexsideoflife31732gut/31732-8.txt.

19. Margaret A. Edwards, *The Fair Garden and the Swarm of Beasts* (New York: Hawthorn Books, 1974), 16.

20. Richard Peck, *The Best Man* (New York: Dial Books for Young Readers, 2016), 60, 68.

21. "*Neuropsychology* journal description," American Psychological Association, 2016, www.apa.org/pubs/journals/neu.

22. International Council for Science, *Position Statement: The Value of Basic Research*, 2004, www.icsu.org/publications/icsu-position-statements/value-scientific-research/the-value-of-basic-scientific-research-dec-2004.

23. See *Stanford Encyclopedia of Philosophy*, s.v. "Critical Theory," by James Bohman, 2005, http://plato.stanford.edu/entries/critical-theory.

24. Danny P. Wallace and Connie van Fleet, *Knowledge into Action: Research and Evaluation in Library and Information Science* (ABC-CLIO, 2012), 99–100; John M. Dawson, "Not Too Academic," *College & Research Libraries* 27, no. 1 (January 1966): 37.

25. Clifford Geertz, "Thick Description: Toward an Interpretive Theory of Culture," in *The Interpretation of Cultures: Selected Essays*, 3–30 (New York: Basic Books, 1973).

26. Curtis Sittenfeld, "I'm on Facebook. It's Over," *New York Times*, September 3, 2011, www.nytimes.com/2011/09/04/opinion/sunday/if-im-on-facebook-it-must-be-over.html?_r=0; Dan Dzombak, "Facebook's Teen Users Down 25% During Past 3 Years," *The Motley Fool*, January 15, 2014, www.fool.com/investing/general/2014/01/15/facebooks-teen-users-down-25-during-the-past-3-yea.aspx; Jennifer Van Grove, "Facebook Fesses Up: Young Teens Are Getting Bored," *CNet*, October 30, 2013, www.cnet.com/news/facebook-fesses-up-young-teens-are-getting-bored; Rachel Rood, "Please Do Not Leave a Message: Why Millennials Hate Voice Mail," *All Tech Considered*, National Public Radio, October 23, 2014, www.npr.org/sections/alltechconsidered/2014/10/23/358301467/please-do-not-leave-a-message-why-millennials-hate-voice-mail.

One

The New Adolescence

R ecent statistics report that more than forty million teens live in the United States. Despite analyses that show this is perhaps 15 percent of the total U.S. population, these numbers represent both a significant population and enormous complexity for young adult librarians. Those responsible for outreach and programming, for developing community partnerships, for responding to reference queries, and for creating appealing and useful collections for teens work amid varied and dynamic contexts. This work is informed by the needs, the interests, and the actual and virtual environments in which young people grow and mature.

Further demographic details about teens can enhance librarians' understanding of this population. If the places teens live are categorized by population density, most live in the suburbs, while 27 percent live in areas regarded as "rural," and 19 percent in urban environments.[1] Substantial numbers of teens live in poverty and experience homelessness; government statistics do not offer figures specific to teens but conclude that slightly more than 20 percent of children seventeen and under have families with incomes below the federal poverty line. These difficulties are higher in ethnic-minority and single-parent households. Patterns of "food insecurity," whether the actual inability to provide food for a family or ongoing fears about the difficulty of doing so, are similar.[2] Data on the rates at which teens complete high school show that increasing numbers of students earn diplomas or equivalent certification, regardless of race.[3] This generation, it has been noted, will see what is sometimes called the *minority majority* phenomenon, in which a plurality of racial and ethnic groups constitute more than 50 percent of the population, spread throughout the country. Researchers at Cornell University observe, "Racial/ethnic diversity is greater in the adolescent population than in the adult U.S. population, and diversity among adolescents is increasing."[4] This trend is confirmed by a 2016 federal report.[5] These figures show that U.S. teens live in a changed and changing world, where there are both successes and setbacks in ensuring their well-being. Demographics, of course, are complicated by contemporary conditions and the way they play out in teens' lives.

Numerous, sometimes conflicting, ideas about American adolescents circulate in the twenty-first century. Teens are said to be technologically adept and capable of electronic multitasking with ease, more immersed in online than actual worlds, promiscuous yet overprotected, overscheduled yet unprepared for school and work, and more. Their youthful virtues and vices receive a fair amount of attention from media outlets and researchers. Not all the resulting contentions about youth cohere, nor do the most attention-getting portrayals always stand up to scrutiny. Some media outlets turn our attention to the extremes of youth culture, and others offer researchers' subtler perspectives on the same activities. Librarians can benefit from understanding and applying research on adolescence in their work with teens.

One fundamental aspect of that research is the definition of *adolescence,* which has to do with cultural roles, rather than age per se. Historian Steven Mintz has observed, "Age is a concept with multiple meanings. It is a chronological marker, a set of sign posts that societies and individuals use to measure their progress through the life course. Age is also a subjective experience."[6] His scholarly commentary on how age functions culturally suggests reasons for the considerable overlap, yet some difference, among the interrelated terms used to categorize the changes long associated in U.S. culture with the teen years. While the Young Adult Library Services Association (YALSA) articulates its commitment to "teens, aged 12–18," other entities focused on young people use different descriptions of this population. For example, *Bright Futures,* produced by Georgetown University's National Center for Education in Maternal and Child Health, defines *adolescence* as the "transition between childhood and adult life."[7] Although *adolescence* and *puberty* have historically overlapped, the two terms refer to different phenomena: the first describes the acquisition of adult roles and responsibilities, while the latter refers to the development of what are, more technically, referred to as secondary sexual characteristics. In recent decades, that development has happened at increasingly younger ages—sometimes as early as eight in girls, according to experts. Meanwhile, researchers who want to better understand brain development have documented its continuation into the mid-twenties in some instances.[8]

If public conversations about teens and adolescents seem confusing, it may be because of the ages now encompassed by *adolescence.* The concerns we have about eight- or even twelve-year-olds are vastly different from those we have about eighteen-year-olds. Untangling these complexities, however, is essential to the work of librarians who must decide where a graphic novel belongs or how to pitch programming at preteens who see themselves as part of a sophisticated, older cohort.

Many librarians acknowledge that, whether because of media reports or actual interactions, our views of adolescence are changing. We think of young people differently in part because teens think of themselves differently. Other forces are at work in changing our ideas about adolescence. Some recent contentions about what it means to be an adolescent in contemporary U.S. society emerged from corporate efforts to sell things to teens. Market researchers in the late twentieth century were among the first to observe that teens' self-concepts, and the purchases that reflected their identities, were changing; they gave this trend the acronym KGOY, which stands for Kids Getting Older Younger. This label reflected the fact that toys once popular with twelve- and thirteen-year-olds were sitting on store shelves. Preteens spurned Barbie as a baby doll and turned their attention and consumer power to things like cell phones and downloaded music. However, researchers with less commercial interests also sought to understand the implications of a maturing and technologically inflected adolescence; these concepts have been slower to enter the marketplace of ideas, less vociferous in contending for our attention.

This book responds to shifting cultural ideas about adolescence by exploring some of the contemporary research that likewise seeks to change the way adolescence is understood. This chapter highlights a few particular claims that are promoted by the media and that will be examined further in the chapters to follow. These ideas might seem counterintuitive, yet recent research indicates that they may help us make sense of the adolescents we work with in our libraries.

MYTH 1

TEENAGERS ARE ESSENTIALLY ADULTS

The idea that a young person who drives, works part-time, and is on the cusp of legal adulthood isn't capable of making certain decisions independently strikes some commentators as incongruous. Yet research in multiple fields indicates that every adolescent isn't exactly an adult-in-waiting. New information about brain development and awareness of changing societal norms are two factors that have influenced researchers' thinking about adolescent development.

Of all the ways that ideas about adolescents are changing, perhaps most significant is the recognition that adolescence is in fact a time of profound change, intellectually and in other respects. Once psychologists believed that teens had acquired fundamental cognitive skills by the time they entered middle school. Now, psychological and sociological research demonstrates that young people acquire adult capabilities at a later age, based on research that has documented extensive brain development during the teen years. It is now accepted that the brain doesn't fully mature until a person is in his midtwenties, because of how the prefrontal cortex, associated with reasoned decision making, develops. As one consumer health site advises, "the rational part of a teen's brain isn't fully developed and won't be until he or she is 25 years old or so."[9] There are individual variations, certainly, and generalizations about how brain development occurs are not meant to imply that teens are incapable of reasoned behavior or thoughtfulness. Instead, many researchers think teens still benefit from active adult involvement in their lives: young people make increasingly challenging decisions while they are in the process of developing reasoning and judgment skills. Researchers and professionals in multiple fields want to better understand the implications of these findings.

Although the research on teens' brain development and associated decision making gets the most attention, sociological observers see the environment in which young people mature as more demanding than it was for past generations. It has been observed that "as young people adapt their lives to a more complex world, it becomes more difficult to say at which point they have reached adulthood. There are more paths to be taken through life and few maps to guide youth on the increasingly complex transition to adulthood."[10] Other researchers, invested in health outcomes, have articulated a Life Course Theory, which looks at a person's experiences "as an integrated continuum rather than as disconnected and unrelated stages."[11] For multiple reasons, then, concepts of adolescence and maturity are becoming extended.

Healthy Communities, Healthy Teens

According to Urban Library Council keynote speaker Dr. Felton Earls of Harvard University, we should envision neighborhoods as "small democracies to produce healthy environments for . . . children to grow up in." Doing so, he argued, helps to ensure adolescents' well-being as they mature. His 2005 remarks highlight the importance of what we now know as community engagement, an increasing focus of professional activity.

One city in particular demonstrates his contentions. "If you want to understand something about human development in urban environments, you have to come to Chicago," Earls said. His research, which shows a complex interaction between neighborhood environments and residents' health, cautions against stereotyping and easy generalizations. Earls and his research team wanted to explain apparently unrelated illness and mortality rates, ultimately finding patterns related to the strength of the community. He noted that socioeconomic factors alone did not account for a "growing disparity" within the city and cited instances of neighborhoods that were poor yet cohesive as well as middle-class neighborhoods experiencing problems related to lack of parental supervision of teens.

Healthy neighborhoods possess a quality Earls refers to as "collective efficacy," meaning that residents work together for their mutual well-being. This feature must be cultivated and supported. "Libraries have to help us stabilize this fragile system of how people become active in their communities," he said, "but young people have to identify themselves as citizens." Helping adolescents realize their potential as healthy, successful individuals, then, means working with communities. ■

MYTH 2

TEENS HATE THEIR PARENTS

When I worked as a young adult librarian, there was a parenting resource book that routinely provoked laughter in the department, called *I'm Not Mad, I Just Hate You*. Although the book focuses on mother-daughter conflict, its title seemed emblematic of all parent-adolescent discord. More recently, a local radio station's interview with a professor, who contends that the rebellion and antagonism against parents that had once been so normal has ebbed, caught my attention. Professor Glenn Gass explained that while he long assumed that all young adults hated their parents' music and rebelled against the choices it represented, conversations with his students taught him the generation in his classrooms these days is different. "I used to think every generation hated their parents and hated their parents' music," he said. Instead, Gass reports, his students tell him, "My best friend's my dad." He concludes that for the young people sometimes labeled millennials, "Music is a real tie to their parents."[12] Despite our sense of recognition when we hear about difficult parent-teen relationships, most problems are not pervasive and the majority of teens see their parents as supportive. Research has shown for many years now that parents enhance their teens' abilities to cope with discomfort during adolescence through what they tell their teens about difficult choices, the information they share, and functioning as role models.

For example, a study about whether young people worry found that when teens confided in their parents, they were less likely to report concerns about peer pressure and popularity. Additionally, teens who talked with their parents reported feeling less worried than those who turned to their peers.[13] Elsewhere, surveys have found that teens do speak with their parents about issues like sexuality and regard them as a preferred source of information about sensitive matters. One recent survey indicated, for example, that only 17 percent of teens "report they use the internet to gather information about health topics that are hard to discuss with others such as drug use and sexual health topics."[14] Similarly, parents have been found to be very influential in the personal decisions teens make, a pattern that has been documented repeatedly in the last decade. Overall, statistics indicate that the vast majority of teens believe they have good relationships with their parents.

This is not a stance recognized broadly within our profession. A library director I interviewed was adamant about the threats parents might pose to their children. She insisted on the need to protect children's borrowing records and other library activities from parents who might not act in their children's best interests. Recognizing that the situation she feared is not typical seems like an important step in understanding the lives of the young people we serve. Librarians need to consider how they might protect children at risk and recognize young people's rights to privacy without assuming all parent-child relationships are troubled ones. Finding ways to encourage or support dialogue between teens and parents would reflect the types of efforts made by other professionals invested in young people's development.

MYTH 3

ADOLESCENTS LEAD UNHEALTHY LIVES

It's not hard for a reasonable individual to suspect that adolescents' health is jeopardized by multiple sources. With their still-developing ability to make sound decisions, they may fail to negotiate difficult situations, such as peer pressure to experiment with drugs or to be a passenger in an intoxicated driver's car. News reporting on the serious problems of bulimia and anorexia abounds, and feminist publications observe with outrage the ways even young girls are targeted by messages about the need to diet and worry about how thin they are. There are, especially in urban communities without easy access to fresh, healthy, and affordable foods, now recognized as "food deserts," diets that increase young people's risk of diabetes through poor food and related weight management problems.

At the same time, though, teens are in good health. Recently released federal statistics show that teen pregnancy rates have dropped, for example.[15] Additionally, most adolescents are insured. They die at lower rates from car accidents, suicide, and homicide than do their slightly older, newly adult peers, while evincing lower rates of drug use, alcohol consumption, and cigarette smoking.[16] While public health professionals continue to strive for gains in all age groups' health and well-being, they find that at least in comparison to those who are only a few years older, teens seem healthier. Enhancing teens' health remains an important goal.

In part, concerns exist because of what researcher Ronald Dahl calls "the paradox of adolescence." He coined the phrase to describe the existence of relatively high rates of injury and death despite other indicators of physical health. Statistics that illuminate the phenomenon show that most deaths among teens aged fifteen to nineteen result from accidents, homicide, and suicide. There is also evidence that 20 percent of U.S. teens are obese, putting them at risk for conditions including heart disease, diabetes, sleep apnea.[17]

MYTH 4

TEENS KNOW TECHNOLOGY BEST

Teens' predilections for technological devices are well documented, yet the question of how well they navigate electronic information remains. While suggested search terms and other developments have aided online searchers with less-than-perfect spelling skills, many issues remain, particularly when it comes to evaluating information. Scholarly studies have repeatedly demonstrated that teens' concentration is fragmented by their efforts to manipulate multiple electronic devices at the same time and that they have weaknesses when it comes to evaluating the materials they retrieve online. While teens may have a facility for text messaging and an inclination to multitask, there are real weaknesses in their technology skills. Librarians' skills and enthusiasm for understanding young people's technological aptitudes are well suited to responding to teens' developing abilities to use the information they obtain electronically.

MYTH 5

WE CAN UNDERSTAND TEENS THROUGH THE MEDIA MARKETED TO THEM

A great deal of writing, past and present, supposes a common youth culture. From Disney and Pixar films to Facebook, it is often assumed that young people consume certain media products that result in a common culture and reflect enthusiasms that aren't necessarily shared by adults. These assumptions are true, up to a point. Researchers have come to recognize that the national and international popularity of works like the Harry Potter series and other top-selling print and digital media is exceptional rather than the rule. There is increasing cause to doubt the extent of tweens' and teens' core entertainment interests.

Increasingly, the nature of the contemporary media market reflects a phenomenon called *segmented programming*—the idea that instead of putting out television programs, for example, that appeal to as broad an audience as possible, programming proliferates so that more specialized programs attract particular kinds of viewers. This practice has become a defining feature of television. In a survey of thousands of middle schoolers, researchers saw little overlap among demographic groups' television preferences. In other words, there were significant differences between the programs girls tended to watch and those favored by boys; further, viewing preferences differed by race as well. The survey's researchers noted, "There is little evidence of a common teen culture across race and gender among adolescents in this sample."[18] In other words, the increasing numbers of minority characters were being seen by other minorities, rather than by white youths, and the on-screen presence of female characters is the focus, primarily, of female teens, not teens of both sexes. Researchers anticipate that the trend toward "bifurcated media worlds" will only grow with the proliferation of new media. We know, for example, that search engine results are not neutral ones, but reflect a number of influences that are grouped under the rubric of "search engine bias."[19] Further, researchers have raised questions about the effect of news provided, for example, via a Facebook feed, where the influence of online friends and their affinities will make certain kinds of stories more visible than others.[20] While these researchers saw portents for the future of multiculturalism in their findings, librarians should note the difficulty of assuming that teen-oriented media reflects broad preferences.

Analysis of teens' use of social-networking sites reveals some key differences. National survey data indicate that "cell phone ownership is nearly ubiquitous among teens and young adults," and the same is true of Internet use.[21] While 55 percent of all U.S. teens had presences on sites like Facebook, site use differed. Older female teens were more likely to have profiles and to maintain connections than were male teens, and they reported that they used online venues to maintain friendships rather than to seek out new ones. Both sexes reported that online flirtation via such sites was relatively rare, and overall, the majority restricted access to their profiles. Still, researchers saw distinct, gender-related preferences in teens' site selections, which they attributed to the extent to which sites reflected real identities and connected to actual geographic locations.[22] The number of teens who use social-networking sites, then, is significant, but so is the number who do not use these much-reported-on sites. Research results also indicate that use of social-networking platforms vary by age and sex, so a young woman's use of Facebook or Twitter may have a different significance than a male peer's use of the same app.

Together, these research findings indicate some of the ways teens differ from one another. Popular media does not translate into universality or even sameness. In seeking cues from popular culture, librarians will want to recognize that they are selecting for the particular teens in their communities, rather than young people writ large.

All indications are that, despite the common ground of youth, teens are distinctively diverse individuals. If they have something in common, it is perhaps that the culture, the choices, and the experiences that shape their lives are different from previous generations and from one another. We can, however, support our interests in engaging contemporary teens with good information about adolescents and adolescence. Dispensing with myths and misperceptions is a starting point for dialogue about the ways librarians can support tweens and teens. Recent population figures suggest we can expect that popular generalizations about their lives will challenge us to understand them as individuals.

FOR FURTHER READING

Federal Interagency Forum on Child and Family Statistics. ChildStats.gov.
    This federation of federal agencies concerned with young people's welfare produces annual reports that provide and interpret national

statistics on people under the age of eighteen. While the forum was founded in 1994, the information presented here is recent rather than historical; contacts for other, more specific data sources are provided.

Pew Research Center. "Teen Fact Sheet." www.pewinternet.org/fact-sheets/teens-fact-sheet.

With references to full reports and updated surveys, this compilation of statistics provides highlights of teens' online activity (in 2012, 95 percent reported connectivity and 81 percent used at least one social-media platform), their views about privacy online, and more. It is a good source for baseline data about contemporary topics and trends.

Shoemaker, Kellie. "Top Ten Myths and Realities of Working with Teen Volunteers." *Voice of Youth Advocates* 21, no. 1 (April 1998): 24–27.

A librarian discusses considerations for working with teens. She advises assessing teens' interest levels and relationships with their parents, as well as coordinating volunteer supervision with other library staff.

NOTES

1. See also ACT for Youth Center of Excellence, "U.S. Teen Demographics, Health, and Behaviors," 2010, https://ecommons.cornell.edu/bitstream/handle/1813/19160/TeenDemographics.pdf?sequence=2&isAllowed=y.
2. Federal Interagency Forum on Child and Family Statistics, *America's Children in Brief: Key National Indicators of Well-Being, 2016* (Washington, DC: U.S. Government Printing Office, 2016), 10, 13, www.childstats.gov/pdf/ac2016/ac_16.pdf.
3. Ibid., 36.
4. ACT for Youth Center of Excellence, "U.S. Teen Demographics."
5. Federal Interagency Forum on Child and Family Statistics, *America's Children in Brief*, 4.
6. Steven Mintz, "Reflections on Age as a Category of Historical Analysis," *Journal of the History of Childhood and Youth* 1, no. 1 (2008): 91–94.

7. Morris Green and Judith S. Palfrey, eds., *Bright Futures: Guidelines for Health Supervision of Infants, Children, and Adolescents,* 2nd edition (Arlington, VA: National Center for Education in Maternal and Child Health, 2002), 231.

8. National Institute of Mental Health "Development of the Young Brain," YouTube video, May 2, 2011, www.nimh.nih.gov/news/media/2011/giedd.shtml; National Institute of Mental Health, "The Teen Brain: Still Under Construction," 2011, https://infocenter.nimh.nih.gov/pubstatic/NIH%2011-4929/NIH%2011-4929.pdf.

9. *University of Rochester Medical Center Health Encyclopedia,* s.v. "Understanding the Teen Brain," www.urmc.rochester.edu/encyclopedia/content.aspx?ContentTypeID=1&ContentID=3051.

10. National Institute for Health Care Management, *Young People's Health Care: A National Imperative* (Washington, DC: National Institute for Health Care Management, 2006), 3. Also available at www.nihcm.org/pdf/YoungPeoplesHCFINAL.pdf.

11. John Richards and Olivia K. Pickett, "Professional Resource Brief: Life Course and Social Determinants," National Center for Education in Maternal and Child Health, May 2015, www.ncemch.org/guides/lifecourse.php.

12. David Johnson, "Rock Historian and Professor Glenn Gass," *Profiles,* WFIU Public Radio, October 31, 2004, www.indianapublicmedia.org/profiles/glenn-gass.

13. S. L. Brown et al., "Gender, Age, and Behavior Differences in Early Adolescent Worry," *Journal of School Health* 76, no. 8 (2006): 430–37.

14. Amanda Lenhart et al., "Social Media and Young Adults," Pew Research Center, February 3, 2010, www.pewinternet.org/2010/02/03/social-media-and-young-adults.

15. "Key Statistics from the National Survey of Family Growth - T Listing," National Center for Health Statistics, 2015, www.cdc.gov/nchs/nsfg/key_statistics/t.htm.

16. National Institute for Health Care Management, *Young People's Health Care,* 8.

17. "Adolescent Health," National Center for Health Statistics, 2015, www.cdc.gov/nchs/fastats/adolescent-health.htm; "Health Problems and Childhood Obesity," Let's Move, www.letsmove.gov/health-problems-and-childhood-obesity.

18. Jane D. Brown and Carol J. Pardun, "Little in Common: Racial and Gender Differences in Adolescents' Television Diets," *Journal of Broadcasting and Electronic Media* 48, no. 2 (June 2004): 272.

19. *Stanford Encyclopedia of Philosophy,* s.v. "Search Engines and Ethics," by Herman Tavani, 2016, http://plato.stanford.edu/entries/ethics-search/#SearEngiBiasProbOpac.

20. Farhad Manjoo, "Facebook's Bias Is Built-In, and Bears Watching," *New York Times,* May 11, 2016, www.nytimes.com/2016/05/12/technology/facebooks-bias-is-built-in-and-bears-watching.html?_r=0.

21. Amanda Lenhart et al., "Social Media and Young Adults."

22. Amanda Lenhart and Mary Madden, "Social Networking Websites and Teens," Pew Research Center, January 7, 2007, www.pewinternet.org/2007/01/07/social-networking-websites-and-teens.

Two

Identity and Community

et me begin by telling you a story about a girl born in a Russian village perhaps one hundred years ago. Her father, a glass blower whose work meant she grew up in a house with windows despite how little money the family had, died when she was in her teens. Her mother believed her chances of marrying again were better if she didn't have a child in her care and left to find a husband in America without her. Their village bordered Poland, and her extended family lived on both sides of it. There was no wall between the two nations, only guards who looked the other way when villagers went into the woods to hunt or forage. One day she arrived at the woodland border with a basket and told them she was going berry picking. Out of sight, she continued to Gdansk, a seaport in Poland. Her journey was one stage of a longer and bigger plan because in those days the United States had barred immigration from Russia. She established residency in

Poland, where visas could be issued for U.S. travel, by living with her uncle, working, and saving money until she could pay for passage on a ship to New York. There she learned English, passed the citizenship test, and met the man who would become her husband, my mother's father, and my grandfather.

I tell you this family history because it suggests facets of identity belied by observation. When people see a white, middle-class professor, the immediate associations are not a grandmother who worked as a cook in a department store or parents who grew up as neighbors to a low-income housing project. I am drawn to interviews with Jennine Capó Crucet, author of *Make Your Home among Strangers,* who describes her experiences as a first-generation college student. Although my mother finished her bachelor's degree the semester before I began mine, I still feel a sense of recognition as she describes the novelties of navigating a residential campus where everyone else seems to know what to do and how to do it.[1] There is more to any person, any library patron, than you can see, and in serving teens, the importance of responding in ways that respect the invisible facets of who they are and who they want to be is paramount.

Identity is both individual and social, how we think about ourselves as people and what aligns us with a group or community. Sex, gender, disability, race, ethnicity, immigration, and socioeconomic status are among the facets that may characterize individuals in the twenty-first century. Sociologist Judith Howard explains, "In current times, the concept of identity carries the full weight of the need for a sense of who one is, together with . . . changes in the groups and networks in which people and their identities are embedded and in the societal structures and practices in which those networks are themselves embedded."[2] Presciently, author Sherman Alexie told an interviewer, "We spend our whole lives asking, Who am I, who am I, who am I? That question is going to have different answers at different times in your life."[3]

His awareness and articulation of identity's mutability are particularly apt to a discussion of adolescence, a time noted for change. A survey of contemporary concerns, followed by discussion of providing library and information services with awareness of these conditions, precedes a snapshot of the historical handling of these matters in the field.

UNDERSTANDING DIVERSITY IN OUR COMMUNITIES

For years, all measures have pointed to an increasingly diverse society. From predictions of a minority majority population to statistics that show one-fourth of the children in this country are classified as immigrants, there are indicators of increasing racial and ethnic diversity in the United States.[4] As we think about the diversity of the young people we serve, we should recognize the diversity of adolescent experience as well: "All cultures recognize and mark the transition from child to adult," yet the conditions of this change are far from universal.[5] While the profession has defined *adolescence* primarily in terms of age, our communities may have their own understandings of what it means to be a young adult, articulated in differing curfews and freedoms. In young adult collections and programming, we need to reflect multiple dimensions of what occurs as youths begin to take on adult roles and responsibilities, the joys and the challenges alike.

One aspect of identity that is often invisible is disability. When cognitive ability and mental health are included, such as dyslexia and depression, there may be no immediate cues that a patron contends with barriers when using our libraries. Yet the most recently available statistics estimate that one in five people in this country live with disability of some sort. Disabilities, particularly physical ones, are more prevalent among senior citizens than among junior and senior high school students.[6] Still, 5 percent of school-aged children in the United States have some sort of disability. Statistical reports suggest that percentage is rarely more than a couple of points higher or lower in any given state, with exceptions such as Maine and Vermont, where the rate is above 8 percent.[7]

Promoting services and resources to individuals in need may prove challenging for multiple reasons. One consideration is the fact that disabilities will vary. In some cases, librarians will aid a person with a disability directly, and in others, they may provide support to parents and caregivers. Evaluating which extant services may benefit library users with disabilities represents a logical starting point; for example, if patrons can request that staff pull items and have them held at a drive-up window, this may be easier for people with mobility limitations. Recently, Teneka Williams argued that, for libraries to address the needs of diverse communities despite proliferating demands and decreasing resources, we have to consider how the tools and strategies for serving one set of needs can work for others too. "We can no longer afford to treat underserved communities as special groups," she writes. "Our communities must be served holistically; we must see the entire community as special."[8] Creating encompassing service plans with an awareness of the differing ways people experience disability and how we can make their library use possible represents a compassionate response. One public library that I visited recently offered an extra open hour to families and children with autism, endeavoring to create a quieter and more soothing environment for those who could be made uncomfortable by crowds and noise.[9]

Marketing such services, however, cannot simply be done by creating a brochure or a website that promotes services to the disabled. An opinion piece in the *New York Times* declares that many individuals do not, collectively, identify as disabled. The author observes that "we have a much clearer collective notion of what it means to be a woman or an African-American, gay or transgender person, than we do of what it means to be disabled. . . . The one thing most people do know about being disabled is that they don't want to be that." Further, and compellingly, the writer notes that disability may not be permanent: "The fact is, most of us will move in and out of disability in our lifetimes, whether we do so through illness, an injury or merely the process of aging."[10] What she suggests is that disability is not only something that has happened to others, but there are real reasons to expect that it could become part of our lives as well. While the author envisions an aging population, for teens, an injury during sports or other activities might create a temporary need for specialized services. Awareness of the ways the library can ensure continuing access or become a new source of recreational activity during such periods, in addition to knowing how to serve ongoing needs, is another dimension of potential service planning.

Another constituency we may not recognize on sight is the LGBTQ community. What we learn about this group of teens depends on where we look for information. Advocacy groups like the Gay, Lesbian and Straight Education Network, PFLAG (officially changed in 2014 from Parents, Families, and Friends of Lesbians and Gays), and the Human Rights Campaign report harm to LGBTQ teens, describing disproportionate amounts of threats, violence, and other kinds of disadvantages.[11] The Centers for Disease Control and Prevention (CDC) offer contrasting information, insisting, "Most lesbian, gay, bisexual, transgender, and questioning youth are happy and thrive during their adolescent years," but that "some LGBTQ youth are more likely than their heterosexual peers to experience difficulties in their lives and school environments, such as violence."[12] Reconciling these disparate judgments involves looking further at the CDC's reporting. It is those who attend "a school that creates a safe and supportive learning environment for all students" and have "caring and accepting parents" who have good lives as teens. Overall, the CDC acknowledges, between 2001 and 2009,

- between 12 and 28 percent of LGBTQ teens were threatened with a weapon at school.
- approximately 20–30 percent experienced violence in an intimate or romantic relationship, and rates of rape are similar.
- "LGBTQ youth are also at increased risk for suicidal thoughts and behaviors, suicide attempts, and suicide."[13]

Recent years have seen the inclusion of material about homosexuality, lesbianism, and questioning one's sexual identity in library collections, but assessments of LGBTQ issues from advocacy groups and the CDC tell us these teens experience numerous difficulties their straight peers don't, from lack of appropriate health care to discrimination and bullying to homelessness.[14] This suggests that beyond including fiction with gay characters, librarians need to provide materials and be prepared to respond to questions about pragmatic, everyday concerns such as medical care and shelter.

This is not necessarily, however, a "build it and they will come" situation. Even if librarians are at ease in responding to questions, patrons may not be entirely comfortable asking them, given cultural, religious, and other norms that make sexuality a charged and private subject. Further, issues have been raised about the efficacy of librarians' responses to adolescents' reference queries on these topics.[15] Looking for ways to ensure teens' privacy in reference interactions, creating visibility of relevant collection materials, and making sure that information to support referrals to shelters or crisis centers is readily available may help ease teens' discomfort with sensitive subjects.

The ways we conceptualize teens' questions about sexuality is far from static, and recognizing changing terminology and emerging issues is necessary if we are to provide accurate information on such sensitive subjects. Now, research and activism call attention to another dimension of sexual identity, often described as nonbinary gender or androgyny in contemporary media accounts and recognized through shifting language choices that avoid once-standard male and female pronouns.[16] A commitment to diversity that respects sexual orientation should respond to the potential information needs of this once little-recognized matter while respecting individuals' privacy, dignity, and personal feelings. In a recent speech, Brian Selznick captured, simply and clearly, some of the fundamental distinctions about terms like *gay* and *queer*. He told his audience,

> *Gay* refers to homosexuality itself. Being gay is being someone attracted to people of the same sex. *Queer* began its life in this context as a slur, used against gay people, a pejorative name to label someone as different, and would be used interchangeably with other slurs. But over time *queer* was appropriated by the very people it was used against, to simultaneously take away the word's sting, while also embracing its ideas of otherness and being an outsider. . . . Over time the use of the word *queer* came to

> mean any kind of questioning of mainstream society's rules and wisdom.[17]

This succinct explanation aside, a library's use of language may still be subject to scrutiny and debate.

Very visible now, because of media and social-media scrutiny, are the ways this country regards race, ethnicity, and immigration status. Challenges to police and civic authority, coupled with a series of court cases restricting the use of affirmative action in university admissions, suggest that the legal terrain for racial issues in this country is changing and may yet see further shifts. Youth services librarians may expect to encounter users whose information needs, perceptions, and feelings are affected by law enforcement and legal rulings, along with public discussion of their merits.

Beyond what we see on the news and in our Facebook feeds, statistics show that books for young people are not keeping pace with the growing proportion of ethnically diverse individuals in this country. Authors whose work begins to fill this gap have recounted their own experiences as young readers and voice the importance of making books with characters of color available to all readers.[18] They also inform us of startling statistics, like data showing that "fully 60 percent of all young black men who drop out of high school will go to jail."[19] Data derived from analysis of the effects of No Child Left Behind legislation have been used to demonstrate that poverty, rather than race alone, may put young people at a disadvantage. Yet research shows that lower socioeconomic status is associated disproportionately with particular ethnic groups. Balancing such findings amid the welter of socioeconomic data available is key to grounding the assumptions that shape our collections, our outreach efforts, and our interactions with younger patrons.

Similarly, other information on young people with ethnic backgrounds demonstrates that while it may seem easy to associate some teens with a particular cultural heritage, teens may see themselves as bicultural. A focus on a Georgia school revealed that Hispanic teens who were inclined to the foods of the region as well as those traditionally associated with their cultural heritage dated teens of other races, and graduated from high school at rates on a par with or higher than other minority groups. As one teen told a reporter, "I live in both worlds."[20] His comment indicates that avoiding stereotypes must extend to recognizing differences within communities as well as the broad ways one culture differs from another.

Diversity and Young Adulthood

Following the publication of *This Is All: The Pillow Book of Cordelia Kenn,* esteemed British author Aidan Chambers offered some provocative ideas about working with young people and books. Speaking at the YALSA President's Program during ALA Annual 2006 in New Orleans, he put forth a number of contentions about young readers and young adult literature, but key to his perspective was the idea that young adult literature ought to encourage teens toward adulthood. "It is admirable to mature," he said, "and the question is, How do we do that?"

Chambers identified two major schools of thought in young adult fiction, one that portrays teen life as authentic and desirable and another that sees it as a transitory and transitional state. He observed that in the United States, the former, which he described as a "thread in teenage literature that valorizes being a teenager . . . and disparages adulthood," has long been dominant. Chambers questioned whether this strain of youth literature supported development into adulthood. Yet classic American literature contains subtle and redeeming models that sympathize with youth while encouraging them to understand a perspective removed from their own, he said.

He argued that, since "life follows art," a fundamental purpose of young adult literature is to represent the transition to adulthood for young readers. Young adult literature, he said, has the potential to help teens work through the puzzles and problems they encounter en route to adulthood. "We are modeling adolescent life to those who read it," he said, and argued that, accordingly, the models we choose for this purpose should be strategic and supportive of teens.

Chambers amused his audience when he argued that the difference between adult and young adult literature is represented by the work of Mark Twain. "The difference to my mind is Huck Finn. Huck Finn pretends to be a teenage consciousness, and it is the consciousness of a bitter, middle-aged man," he said, stating that the consciousness of the elder informs the younger. "They are looking at how to figure things out," Chambers said of young readers. "How will we know what to do? Only if life models art." Although his words were light, his point was serious.

By arguing categorically against adolescence he confronted questions about how to connect young people and books and how to identify books with youth appeal. "There is no such thing as an adolescent," Chambers said. "It is a state in life. They are as diverse as we are." These ideas challenge librarians to consider the adolescent as an individual rather than a member of a cohort with particular characteristics. They suggest that for every video-game-playing teen there is a quiet reader, or that the gamer may even want reading material that might seem to be at odds with her screen-involved persona. Instead of thinking of youth appeal in reductive terms in order to make easy connections between resources and young people, Chambers presents the need to consider each young person as a complex and sophisticated individual. ■

DIVERSE CULTURES AND LIBRARIES' INFORMATION CLIMATES

The way we define our collections for young people has consequences for our efforts to serve diverse audiences. Research points to areas of concern in collection management and service to young people of different backgrounds. Some of those findings are highlighted here. The notion of adolescence as a time of transition, in particular, seems valuable in this context, invoking change and multiple aspects of identity rather than emphasizing a fixed idea of what it means to be a teen.

One researcher has argued that the digital divide is not simply a matter of access to electronic information resources, but a larger problem with how web-based resources represent people of color.[21] Developed in the context of online news in the wake of Hurricane

Katrina, the essential questions this researcher raised are worth considering in the ongoing context of our work with young people too. If the available materials are implicitly racist or present distorted perceptions of ethnic issues, their value to any user is questionable. For an individual who identifies with a group misrepresented in library resources, this constitutes another barrier to information use.

In efforts to respond to young people's interests, youth collections feature materials that libraries once categorically rejected. Yet thinking of chart-topping contemporary music, popular magazines, and certain kinds of electronic resources as the core of a young adult collection has the potential to flatten our sense of what it means to be a teen in the twenty-first century. Despite the genuine appeal these materials hold for many young people, researchers have begun to indicate that the adolescent media market is in fact more segmented than commonly believed.

While striving to understand demographics and group attributes, it's important not to lose sight of the actual library user. Understanding general features of diversity cannot replace dialogue and expressed needs. At the risk of oversimplifying matters, I would argue that information is an important component of effective planning for service to diverse youth populations. Obtaining information from reliable sources that can speak to the particulars of the local or regional situation has the potential to clarify actual community needs. Due to reporting requirements, school districts that regularly generate data about race, ethnicity, poverty, and community changes may be effective partners in surveying the local area. Information derived from empirical research does not always support commonly held perceptions about young people. Both the individual and demographic norms must be considered.

Critically, most proponents of effective outreach to diverse communities note the importance of talking with members of the community to construct authentic notions of their values and their needs. For example, retired library director Glen Holt differentiates between offering services to the poor and serving the poor—between making services available should someone who is poor take the initiative to come to the library and constructing services to address the conditions in which impoverished people actually live. In this context, young people who have homework and who are gaining literacy skills can find themselves at a disadvantage, not because of issues like computer access but because of bureaucracies that fail to communicate with parents in ordinary language and policies that penalize those who can least afford additional costs. Making young people from poor families welcome if they come to you is not the same, Holt argues, as actively conducting outreach using meaningful strategies and developing policies that acknowledge barriers to library use that affect poor families unfairly.[22]

CONCLUSION

The aspects of identity that are of interest continue to shift with time. What cannot change is our determination to look past the obvious, to serve and support the individuals in our communities regardless of how they understand and describe themselves. James Baldwin's sentiments seem apt in the here and now: "I was not born to be what someone said I was. I was not born to be defined by someone else, but by myself, and myself only."[23] Baldwin's insistence on the affirmative aspects of identity and the prerogative of self-definition reminds us that some community members will have experienced the burden of confronting others' expectations—and that goodwill may not be enough to make them feel welcome and at ease in our libraries.

There are myriad aspects of identity that might cause individuals to feel at odds with the surrounding culture or to experience discrimination. How we think about our users with these traits affects the way we develop and maintain resources for them. In some ways, identity as described here is equated with difference, with things that might create challenges for individuals. Recognizing teens' vulnerabilities doesn't mean seeing them as victims, though adolescence is a time when people are more prone to life-altering difficulties. One library director has written about a new initiative that helps at-risk teens through two different peer-outreach efforts, believing that teens are best positioned to recognize when others their age need help.[24]

Though libraries, like other institutions, have struggled to change with the times, exemplary librarians have sought to serve young and old, regardless of race. Margaret Edwards, who used horse-drawn wagons to get materials to the residents of poor, inner-city Baltimore neighborhoods, became recognized as an exemplar of outreach, and her work with Baltimore's African-American population stands as another of her progressive efforts to serve those whom libraries once excluded.[25] The roughly contemporary story of Oklahoman Ruth Brown, who purchased series fiction and looked the other way when students engaged in a then-shocking display of public affection by holding hands, ended differently. Brown's efforts to provide equitable, user-centered services in an interracial community resulted in her 1950 dismissal from the Bartlesville Public Library, not many years before ALA issued its Freedom to Read Statement.[26] Brown lacked a champion in her contemporaries, and her story reminds us that even if we succeed locally, we may have colleagues elsewhere who could benefit from our support.

At present, there is no shortage of guidance on the ideals of library service for all users. ALA has statements and policies on more than forty different topics, at least four of which clearly pertain to young people.[27] Nearly all of these official pronouncements explicitly concur in the importance of valuing ethnic, racial, and other backgrounds. Few statements advise librarians how to achieve these goals, particularly when it comes to the sensitive matter of minors, young people with limited rights and in legal relationships with adults who are entitled to make decisions concerning the actions of youth under the age of eighteen. Librarians who serve this younger and increasingly diverse generation will find themselves working continuously to understand community demographics and personal identity so they can respond with meaningful services.

FOR FURTHER READING

Cart, Michael, and Christine Jenkins. *The Heart Has Its Reasons: Young Adult Literature with Gay/Lesbian/Queer Content*. Lanham, MD: Scarecrow Press, 2006.

> This volume offers critical commentary on the changing ways LGBTQ themes have been presented in YA literature, along with reading lists for teens and bibliographies of secondary sources on the subject. A revised and updated edition is in preparation.

Coates, Ta-Nehisi. *Between the World and Me*. New York: Spiegel and Grau, 2015.

> Crafted as an open letter to his teenage son, this volume has received significant critical notice and awards, including the National Book Award. It is a meditation, alternately painful and powerful, on the history of race relations in the United States. Coates questions the notion of race except as a construct that rationalizes harm to African-Americans. His fundamental observation revolves around "the vulnerability of the black teenage bodies" (15). Coates writes, "When I was your age, each day, fully one-third of my brain was concerned with who I was walking to school with, our precise number, the manner of our walk . . . which is to say that I practiced the culture of the streets, a culture chiefly concerned with securing the body" (24). The resulting and enduring fear, he states, is "a great injustice" (28). He calls love "an act of heroism" (60), encouraging his son to become "a conscious citizen of this terrible and beautiful world" (108). He recalls his self-directed learning in the Moorland archives at Howard University, writing, "The library was open, unending, free" (48). Coates does not offer pat answers to problems or optimistic, idealistic visions as he describes change and constancy in the experience of African-Americans.

Curry, Ann. "If I Ask, Will They Answer? Evaluating Public Library Reference Service to Gay and Lesbian Youth." *Reference and User Services Quarterly* 45, no. 1 (Fall 2005): 65–75.

An unobtrusive study of inquiries at the reference desk by a female teen seeking information related to gay and lesbian issues garnered mixed results. The teen proxy who asked for information rated librarians on approachability, comfort levels during the reference interview, and appropriateness of responses to her questions. Curry describes behaviors and utterances the teen found welcoming as well as those that suggested disapproval or discomfort.

Kuklin, Susan. *Beyond Magenta: Transgender Teens Speak Out.* Somerville, MA: Candlewick Press, 2014.
Six profiles of transgender adolescents express their perspectives and experiences of navigating school, family, and social relationships along with changes in their sense of self and bodies during the teen years. For librarians who take seriously the idea that all users should see themselves reflected in the collection, this sometimes difficult book, now found on ALA's list of frequently challenged titles, would be a valuable resource. It includes a glossary and a list of resources for research and support.

Library Anchor Models for Bridging Diversity Achievement. *LAMBDA Project.* http://lambda.sis.utk.edu.
This is a continuing education effort that helps libraries better serve LGBTQ teens, with links to resources for librarians and teens from the site, including some specific to each state. Slides with facts, consciousness-raising exercises, and related information from experts' presentations are also accessible.

Naidoo, Jamie Campbell, and Sarah Park Dahlen. *Diversity in Youth Literature: Opening Doors through Reading.* Chicago: ALA Editions, 2013.
Covering children's and young adult collections, this volume is a primer on diversity in library materials. It also discusses reflecting race and ethnicity, as well as sexual identity, in library holdings.

Tyson, Timothy B. *Blood Done Sign My Name: A True Story.* New York: Crown Books, 2004.
Although not about libraries, this powerful, award-winning narrative provides a striking perspective on race issues and the

civil rights movement in the American South. Used by a number of libraries and partner organizations as a One Community, One Book selection, Tyson's autobiographical investigation of a black man's murder is, as one commentator has observed, a reminder that "changes in race relations have not come about peacefully or quickly" and that "much remains to be done."[28] Informal commentaries posted on the Web insist that everyone should read this book, and this reader agrees.

University of Iowa. "Resources for Trans Communities and Their Allies." https://uiowa.edu/ui-trans-resources/.

A new resource created for the Iowa community, this site both offers broadly applicable information, such as a primer on pronouns, and models useful information that other entities might want to provide, like a map marking the locations of "single-use, gender-inclusive restrooms" around campus. The list of supporting organizations begins with local and state groups but also links to national ones that respond to general and specific needs, such as the Transgender American Veterans Association.

NOTES

1. "Novel Highlights the Shocks Facing First-Generation College Students," *All Things Considered,* radio broadcast, National Public Radio, August 8, 2015, www.npr.org/2015/08/08/430044277/novel-highlights-the-shocks -facing-first-generation-college-students.

2. Judith A. Howard, "Social Psychology of Identities," *Annual Review of Sociology* 26 (2000): 367–93, www.uvm.edu/pdodds/files/papers/ others/2000/howard2000a.pdf.

3. Jason Morgan Edwards, "A Conversation with Sherman Alexie About Thunder Boy Jr. and Other Stuff," *Indian Country Today Media Network,* June 25, 2016, http://indiancountrytodaymedianetwork .com/2016/06/25/conversation-sherman-alexie-about-thunder-boy-jr -and-other-stuff-164925.

4. Lesli A. Maxwell, "U.S. School Enrollment Hits Majority-Minority Milestone," *Education Week* (August 19, 2014), www.edweek.org/ew/ articles/2014/08/20/01demographics.h34.html; "Protecting Immigrant Children," American Academy of Pediatrics, 2016, www.aap.org/en-us/ advocacy-and-policy/federal-advocacy/Pages/ImmigrationReform.aspx.

5. "Population Reports: Meeting the Needs of Young Adults," *Family Planning Programs,* ser. J, no. 41 (October 1995): 3.

6. U.S. Census Bureau, "Nearly 1 in 5 People Have a Disability in the U.S., Census Bureau Reports," news release, July 25, 2012, www.census.gov/ newsroom/releases/archives/miscellaneous/cb12-134.html.

7. U.S. Census Bureau, "School-Aged Children with Disabilities in U.S. Metropolitan Statistical Areas: 2010," *American Community Survey Briefs (*November 2011), 1, 4, www.census.gov/prod/2011pubs/acsbr10 -12.pdf.

8. Teneka Williams, "On My Mind: Inclusivity in Any Library," *American Libraries* 47, no. 6 (June 2016): 28.

9. Genevieve Trainor, "Iowa City Autism Group Plans 'Browsing Hour' at the Library," *Little Village Magazine,* September 16, 2016, http:// littlevillagemag.com/iowa-city-autism-group-plans-browsing-hour-at -the-library.

10. Rosemarie Garland-Thomson, "Becoming Disabled," *New York Times,* August 19, 2016, www.nytimes.com/2016/08/21/opinion/sunday/ becoming-disabled.html?_r=0.

11. "Statistics You Should Know About Gay & Transgender Students," PFLAG New York City, 2015, www.pflagnyc.org/safeschools/statistics; "Growing Up LGBT in America: View Statistics," Human Rights Campaign, 2012, 2015, www.hrc.org/youth/view-statistics/ #.Vktwp5NVhHx.

12. "LGBT Youth," National Center for HIV/AIDS, Viral Hepatitis, STD, and TB Prevention, 2014, www.cdc.gov/lgbthealth/youth.htm.

13. Ibid.; also see "Youth Risk Behavior Surveillance System," Division of Adolescent and School Health, 2016, www.cdc.gov/healthyyouth/data/ yrbs/index.htm/.

14. Mark A. Schuster et al., "A Longitudinal Study of Bullying of Sexual-Minority Youth," *New England Journal of Medicine (*May 7, 2015), doi:10.1056/NEJMc1413064; "Research," True Colors Fund, 2016, https://truecolorsfund.org/our-work/research/; C. Winter, *Responding to LGBT Health Disparities,* Missouri Foundation for Health, August 2012, www.mffh.org/wordpress/wp-content/uploads/2016/04/ LGBTHealth Equity Report.pdf; Lambda Legal, National Alliance to End Homelessness, nn4y, and National Center for Lesbian Rights, "National Recommended Best Practices for Serving LGBT Homeless Youth," www.lambdalegal.org/sites/default/files/publications/downloads/ bkl_national-recommended-best-practices-for-lgbt-homeless-youth _0.pdf.

15. Jennifer Chance Cook, "GLBTQ Teen Literature: Is It Out There in Indiana?" *Indiana Libraries* 23, no. 2 (2004): 25–28; Ann Curry, "If I Ask, Will They Answer? Evaluating Public Library Reference Service to Gay and Lesbian Youth," *Reference and User Services Quarterly* 45, no. 1 (Fall 2005): 65–75.

16. An overview of the history of gendered and un-gendered pronouns in English from 1792 to 2015 is available online: Dennis Baron, "The Words that Failed: A chronology of early nonbinary pronouns," www.english .illinois.edu/-people-/faculty/debaron/essays/epicene.htm.

17. Brian Selznick, "Love Is a Dangerous Angel: Thoughts on Queerness and Family in Children's Books," Arbuthnot honor lecture, Children & Libraries Conference, Washington, DC, Winter 2015, sp. 5, www .youtube.com/watch?v=0daG_vcZaJo.

18. Grace Lin, "The Windows and Mirrors of Your Child's Bookshelf," TED video of presentation, TEDxNatick, Natick, MA, January 2016, http:// tedxtalks.ted.com/video/The-Windows-and-Mirrors-of-Your; Jacqueline Woodson, *Brown Girl Dreaming* (New York: Nancy Paulsen Books, 2014); and "Jacqueline Woodson: By the Book," *New York Times,* August 25, 2016, www.nytimes.com/2016/08/28/books/review/jacqueline -woodson-by-the-book.html.

19. Ta-Nehisi Coates, *Between the World and Me* (New York: Spiegel and Grau, 2015), 27.

20. Rachel L. Swarns, "Hispanic Teenagers with Outsider Roots Are Finding a Way In," *New York Times,* December 31, 2006, A16.

21. André Brock, "A Belief in Humanity Is a Belief in Colored Men: Using Culture to Span the Digital Divide," *Journal of Computer-Mediated Communication* 11, no. 1, article 17 (2005), http://jcmc.indiana.edu/ v0111/issue1/brock.html.

22. Glen E. Holt, "Fitting Library Services into the Lives of the Poor," *Bottom Line* 19, no. 4 (2006): 179–86.

23. Quoted in Rona Cran, "Multifaceted," *Times Literary Supplement,* November 20, 2015, 5.

24. Misty Jones, "Out of the Shadows," *American Libraries* (June 2016): 24.

25. Margaret Edwards, *The Fair Garden and the Swarm of Beasts* (New York: Hawthorn Books, 1969), 50–62.

26. Louise Robbins, *The Dismissal of Miss Ruth Brown,* new ed. (Norman: University of Oklahoma Press, 2001); American Library Association and Association of American Publishers, *The Freedom to Read Statement,* June 30, 2004, www.ala.org/advocacy/intfreedom/statementspols/ freedomreadstatement.

27. "Intellectual Freedom Statements and Policies," American Library Association, 2016, www.ala.org/Template.cfm?Section=censorship &template=/ContentManagement/ContentDisplay.cfm&ContentID =114327.

28. Susan Garrett, quoted in "Memoir about Racially Motivated Murder Earns International Religion Award," press release, Grawemeyer Foundation at University of Louisville, December 1, 2006, www .grawemeyer.org/news-updates/religion07.html (site discontinued).

Three

Sex and Sexualities

riting for teens, writing about teens, and writing by teens contribute to a sense that twenty-first-century adolescents lead lives inflected by sexuality.[1] Of course, this shouldn't be surprising because puberty and adolescence coincide. Researchers tell us that "the development of sexuality is one of the most salient aspects of adolescence" and "the initiation of romantic relationships represents a key developmental task of adolescence."[2] Teen romance is important in its own right because "high-quality, satisfying romantic relationships are linked to healthy development during adolescence and can set the stage for successful relationships into adulthood."[3] It follows, then, that romance, sexuality, and reproductive health are normal aspects of adolescence and library collections developed for adolescents. The collections and the information they offer matter to adults as well as adolescents. The Sexuality Information and Education Council of the United States observes,

> As they grow and mature, young people need access to accurate information about their sexuality. And parents, educators, and policymakers need information about young people's knowledge, attitudes, and behaviors in order to support them and provide high quality educational opportunities.[4]

Certainly librarians are also a group of people who need this context.

Whether the topic is sexual activity or abstinence, there is much cultural and research attention to this dimension of teens' lives, and what it means to provide an accurate, sensitive, and welcoming information environment is increasingly shifting. We might have thought ourselves reasonably progressive, even ten years ago, by making available straightforward information about reproductive biology and YA novels that acknowledge teens' sexuality, but today the cultural and political climate of our country and the new voices on LGBTQ issues have greatly increased our awareness of what is possible and what is at stake when we talk about adolescent sexuality. It is a dynamic, even turbulent, time. During the writing of this chapter, the terrain shifted repeatedly. One week, I bookmarked a snippet of President Barack Obama's speech during LGBT Pride Month, in which he proclaimed that discrimination was "so last century" and a news report on an Oregon court's ruling that the state's residents can legally declare their gender nonbinary.[5] Now I write as details of the largest mass shooting in modern U.S. history, a violent act that targeted a gay nightclub in Orlando, Florida, unfold. Victims were as young as eighteen, and one worked at the popular Harry Potter theme park.[6] In the time since the shooting, some Orlando-area individuals have felt compelled to act in hopes of improving conditions for the LGBTQ community, and their work includes a focus on teens. One counselor has dedicated herself to forming new "gay-straight alliances in schools and . . . support for existing ones" to commemorate a friend killed that night, and a transgender teen has come forward with his stories of bullying at school contrasted with his mother's "open arms to come home to." He heads an advocacy group that works to redress bullying and conditions that make school difficult for LGBTQ teens.[7] The tandem advances and threats form part of the context in which adolescents mature and make choices.

This chapter offers an overview of recent research on teens and sex, accompanied by the analysis of interdisciplinary experts. Although the political and legal situation shifts with each election and court decision, some background on the current, if controversial, public conversation about sexual identity foregrounds this discussion. An overview of selected terminology that reflects different dimensions of sexual identity is also part of this chapter, as is recent statistical information on teen sexuality. Finally, consideration of selected titles and key facets of the literature on library services and related issues concludes this chapter. These topics, I hope, offer librarians serving young people a context for services, including collection management, that engage varied dimensions of sex and sexuality.

WHEN WE TALK ABOUT SEX
New Contexts and Changing Terms

News stories illuminate the issues surrounding sexuality in the twenty-first century. Some are specific to teens, while others affect them as citizens of the nation and of the world, creating openings for or restrictions on their ability to be the people they are becoming. The BBC, for example, reported the death of a transgender activist in Pakistan, when she was shot and medical practitioners failed to provide timely and appropriate care.[8] In the United States, Republicans in the House of Representatives have voted down two different bills that would protect LGBTQ federal employees from being fired on the basis of their sexual identity.[9] Prior to the most recent vote, President Obama's administration issued a directive to U.S. public schools requiring that they allow students to use restrooms and locker rooms per their own sense of self.[10] In a news report on the administration's decision, John B. King Jr. was quoted as saying, "We must ensure that our young people know that whoever they are and wherever they come from, they have the opportunity to get a great educa-tion in an environment free from discrimination, harassment and violence."[11] Despite the laudable aims of equity and safety, to date, attorneys general from twelve states have filed lawsuits challenging the executive order.

In the midst of this political and legal environment, ALA and many U.S. libraries have endeavored to support the patrons and staff whom these policy actions seek to protect. Well before the controversy over access to public restrooms unfolded, *American Libraries* shared the ideas of "librarians [who] are expanding their safe spaces to include bathrooms, specifically gender-neutral restrooms for patrons who identify as transgender or gender nonconforming."[12] NYPL has a history of supporting LGBTQ teens by hosting an "anti-prom" since 2004, offering a space where teens can socialize without worrying about whether they conform to popular ideas about proms.[13] The year 2016 brought news that the 2006 Printz award winner *Looking for Alaska* led ALA's list of most frequently challenged books, with complainants objecting to its "offensive language" and "sexually explicit descriptions."[14] More than once author John Green has responded to adults who call *Looking for Alaska* either salacious or too mature for teens, saying his book confounds the idea that casual sex is desirable.[15] ALA's Office for Intellectual Freedom was among the groups that responded to the most recent challenge, insisting that its subject matter and "'characters who talk smart, yet don't always behave that way'" were the very traits that prove the novel "deserves its place in the classroom and on the library shelf."[16] These examples show that, while library history is filled with examples of censorship in difficult times and closed-minded responses to difference, in the twenty-first century libraries are working to ensure that the record they leave does not repeat earlier weaknesses and limitations.

Finally, it is easy to focus on the aspects of sex that are making headlines here and around the world. We must remember, however, that our communities include teens who, for reasons including personal faith, express their sexual identity through chastity and abstinence. Teens may attend private schools that encourage these choices. A friend's middle-school-aged daughter delighted in telling me, with only mild eye rolling, about attending dances where school administrators would caution couples who danced too closely to "make room for the Holy Spirit" between them. Although she found the rules overly cautious, she wasn't angered by or defiant of them. A recent Pew Research Center study of young adults' religious beliefs found that, while fewer young people than in the past affiliate with particular religious denominations, many still believe and accept moral precepts associated with church teachings.[17] Respecting and responding to the varied perspectives of young adults in our communities means balancing multiple demands and information sources.

Of all the young people we serve, how we talk with and about those whose attractions inspired the phrase "Love is love" may prove most challenging. There are several guides to language and labels for people whose choices are sometimes doubted and contested, and there is individual preference. I have, for instance, seen a gay student grow upset over terms used in a book widely praised for its sensitive and sympathetic approach to sexual identity. Although I will highlight the array of terminology for sexual identity here, along with commentaries that explore the meaning and significance of these terms, the bottom line seems to be that one should ask, rather than assume, when these matters factor in conversation.

For decades, the words *sex* and *gender* have been used to differentiate between a certain kind of body and the cultural associations and expectations that accrue to it. Numerous issues, including growing awareness of intersex bodies and transsexual identity, complicate distinctions between biology and culture. Other related considerations have to do with how we talk about attraction and intimacy.

One of the first documents where I saw an expansive list of terms describing sexual identity was the Nerdfighteria Census for 2015. I had seen words like *queer* in the news and in scholarly essays, including one in the *Chronicle of Higher Education* that pronounced the demise of queer studies, and lesbian students in a seminar had explained the meaning of terms like *cisgender,* a descriptor for individuals whose gender identity matches their birth sex, which *Urban Dictionary* tells us may be "used derogatively."[18] Even with eleven categories to choose from, survey respondents were still given the option of declaring that these labels didn't suit them and providing their own, as if in response to a young person who once asked, according to the *New York Times,* "Why do only certain letters get to be in the full acronym?"[19] Researchers have pursued this question from a more theoretical perspective. As one wrote in a peer-reviewed journal, "the conventional conceptualization of sexual orientation has a number of shortcomings. Indeed, why would the sex of our desired partners be the prime organizing feature of our sexuality? What is the role of partners' genderedness or of other major person characteristics?"[20] These questions reflect a conversation about sexual identity that is still taking place.

It is a conversation, research suggests, that young teens are likely to feel themselves a part of. Recent research on sexual attraction found that at thirteen, young people's preferences tended to be fluid rather than fixed and sometimes didn't represent their adult identity. More technically, "Although same-sex romantic attractions emerge early, they are typically non-exclusive in early adolescence and they differ from later same-sex orientations."[21] While the survey has its limitations, it suggests that young teens are aware of their sexuality and acknowledge same-sex as well as opposite-sex attraction, rather than one or the other.

Library resources on gay identity contain multiple variations on the *LGBTQ* acronym, among them *LGBTQIA*, where the letters stand for lesbian, gay, bisexual, transgender, questioning or queer, intersex, and ally or asexual. At times, a plus sign follows to acknowledge other ways of characterizing one's feelings about sex and the body. The *New York Times* called this construct emerging in 2013, as it identified some two hundred colleges and universities that "allow transgender students to room with their preferred gender" and approximately fifty where students can officially change their names and genders in university records.[22] At that time, use of the longer term, *LGBTQIA*, was becoming seen as evidence of both a younger generation's sensibilities and a "more progressive outlook."[23] It is the prevailing approach, though there are numerous alternatives, including *GSM*, which stands for gender and sexual minorities. Each of the variant initialisms and acronyms attempts to be either more precise or more inclusive in its construction of gender and sexual identity, but no revision has prevented some from asking whether all the individuals clustered by such terminology in fact share common concerns and values.[24]

A *Washington Post* opinion piece outlined the "ever-changing acronym" and its implications. Arguing that the words *lesbian* and *gay* carry, at this point, readily evident meanings, author Ryan Carey-Mahoney says that they replace words like *homosexual,* which was once an APA *Diagnostic and Statistical Manual of Mental Disorders* entry. Medical and psychiatric use of the word to characterize emotions and acts as problems that could be cured through treatment means it is in disfavor among members of the LBGT community.[25] Some individuals accept *gay* as a reference to both men and women, while some maintain that it is a term that describes men only.

The *Washington Post* article presents the idea that bisexuality has long been misunderstood as a precursor to or a transition point in an individual's adoption of a gay or lesbian identity. It also offers a concise explanation of the ways that the letters in the commonly used acronym represent different aspects of identity, with some elements reflecting romantic choices and others a sense of selfhood: "While the first three letters (LGB) focus on sexual identity, transgender refers to a person's gender identity, namely that they don't identify with the gender they were born into." The latter individuals may either identify with a gender other than the one that they were born to or voice a preference for gender neutrality, often expressed through the use of collective or plural pronouns, like *they* and *theirs,* rather than conventionally singular pronouns that connote gender.

A living language changes to reflect culture and innovation. How we talk about sex, gender, and love has shifted to signal the feelings and the preferences of communities that react to words used to belittle and exclude them. Although aimed more at tweens than teens, the award-winning book *George* by Alex Gino models language and messages that signal acceptance of a transgender individual's feelings and choices.[26] For those of us who remember the rules of usage iterated in our English classes, where singular nouns combined with plural pronouns resulted in red-inked corrections, these changes may feel awkward. Making library users feel welcome, though, means learning new expressions and ideas to respond to the way our users see themselves.

STUDYING TEEN SEXUALITY
Statistical Reports and Policy Publications

What do entities collecting information on teens and sex tell us? Their surveys reveal a number of facts about teen sexuality and, equally important, how those facts change with time and place. *Are fewer teens having sex? Do they use condoms? Are the teens I know like the ones I'm hearing about via the news?* These are the sorts of questions that large-scale studies of adolescents address. Such studies say, broadly speaking, that approximately half of U.S. high school students acknowledge having had "at least one sexual experience."[27] Learning more, as well as why it matters, involves assessing numerous studies and expert commentaries.

It is easy to be skeptical of statistics and of information released on behalf of an administration whose politics may differ from our own or by advocacy groups we believe to be extreme. Even highly qualified researchers issue caveats about our ability to understand adolescent sexuality without revising our perspectives and the questions we ask. Consider, for example, the observations of Deborah L. Tolman, who stated that "several studies have shown that by 9th grade, 25% of girls, on average, have had sexual intercourse in this country. Whether they wanted to have this experience, why, and what it meant to them, is data that has never been collected."[28] Statistics cannot reveal everything, but when collected and analyzed appropriately, they can provide reliable information about the phenomena they were designed to measure. In the case of teen sexuality, national statistics indicate varying rates of sexual activity by factors such as age, sex, and ethnicity as well as reveal changes in behavior and outcomes such as pregnancy. More focused surveys now offer insights into teens' attitudes and actions that were once unexamined.

A number of government agencies and nongovernmental organizations (NGOs) gather and provide statistical information about teens and sex. Entities like the CDC and the National Institutes of Health in the federal government and the Guttmacher Institute in the private sector conduct surveys over multiple years to gather evidence of trends. Some undertake relatively rare and expensive large-scale data collection on sexuality to gather information that could not be obtained with fewer resources. They are able to obtain confidential information because individual details become part of a statistical composite that cannot be linked to one person or even one community. The office administering the Youth Risk Behavior Surveillance System (YRBSS) explicitly identifies the preservation of respondents' confidentiality as the chief reason "YRBSS data are not available by zip code, census tract, or school."[29] Regardless of the agendas of these bodies, the statistical information they offer on sexuality is of value in understanding teens.

Typically, these government offices and associations develop data about how many teens are sexually active and related matters with the intent of examining the figures for their policy implications. For example, if teens are sexually active but a substantial subset of this group does not use birth control, questions about who they are and the reasons for their behaviors are of interest. Some entities will be concerned about projected budgets for social and health services for this population, while others will want to know more in order to do outreach and communication about preventing pregnancy in teens who have yet to finish high school or take steps toward other major goals that will determine the courses of their lives. While there is a shared interest in understanding teen sexual activity, motives and intended uses for gathering information vary.

A starting point for statistics on sex is the most recent survey data, accepted by multiple sources, that indicate approximately half of U.S. teens age fifteen and older either are or have been sexually active. According to the CDC, this represents a significant decrease from the numbers reported since 1990. It is worth noting that the questionnaire used in this survey does not ask teens to identify the sex or gender of their partners. The same resource informs us that between 79 and 84 percent of teens who have had sex report using birth control.[30]

A related trend is a small but continuing decline in the teen birth rate; still, experts observe that the number of U.S. teens having children before they are eighteen is one of the highest in industrialized nations, and ethnic minorities are disproportionately represented in these statistics. The concern is not with teens' morals, but their well-being, a further cultural change. As the research and advocacy group Child Trends explains, "Teen childbearing is linked to a host of negative outcomes among teen mothers, their children, and society as a whole."[31] Everything from how much money teen parents make to health status is affected, most often negatively, by teen pregnancy, and this drives policy concerns about teens' sexual activity. Thus, if librarians pursue further facts in the medical and public health literature, they are likely to see references to teens' risky behavior. In this context, risk is a sort of shorthand for the greater likelihood of poverty and lower education levels for teenage parents and their children.

Other research that looks for patterns in the relationships of couples between the ages of eighteen and twenty-five found that 20 percent of young adults were dating, married to, or living with a person of a different cultural or ethnic background.[32] While this population is slightly older than most of the teens who seek services at YA desks, the trend is believed to be broadly representative. Fifty years after the Supreme Court overturned laws that criminalized interracial marriage (*Loving v. Virginia,* 388 U.S. 1), these intimate relationships are emblematic of subsequent cultural change.

It is harder to find official statistics that project how many teens might identify as lesbian, gay, bisexual, or transgender, and research suggests that attitudes as well as attraction figure in recent estimates. Groups like the Gay, Lesbian and Straight Education Network (GLSEN) and PFLAG typically extrapolate from the percentage of gays and lesbians in the population as a whole to indicate the number of teens.[33] This reasoning suggests, then, that between 4 and 10 percent of the younger population are assumed to be interested or involved in same-sex relationships. At the same time, one newspaper headline reports, "Same-Sex Experiences Are on the Rise, and Americans Are Increasingly Chill About It." This interpretation of a scholarly research project finds that "the percentage of men reporting male sexual partners had nearly doubled from 1999 to 2014, and the percentage of women reporting same sex partners had *more than* doubled during the same period" (emphasis original).[34] The researchers said their data reflect both a younger generation—the so-called millennials—that is more accepting and a general shift in social attitudes.[35] The study's figures, however, remain within the statistical estimates offered by advocacy groups, clustering toward the upper end of that range.

Expert opinion and survey data indicate that there are differences between young adults' actions and ideas about sexuality and that adolescent sexuality is sometimes associated with negative outcomes. For these and other reasons, adolescent sexuality is a broad object of interest, and providing information about teen sex should be informed by empirical research as well as professional ideals. The research literature in LIS represents a tiny portion of what we know about teens, sex, and related information-seeking behaviors. In part because they typically work with larger, more representative samples, rather than a handful of interview participants, researchers in cognate fields offer much sound, verifiable knowledge about how teens regard messages about birth control, their health-information seeking, and rates of homelessness among LGBTQ teens. These studies offer clues about what information teens might need and can enhance our ability to connect them with resources that might make a difference in their lives.

Three key surveys provide statistics and explanatory comments that can help youth services librarians understand recent trends in teen sexual behavior. As we seek information that informs us of changes in our communities and as we evaluate media reports and advocacy groups' contentions, the results of these key surveys allow us to gauge the currency and the generalizability of what we hear. Although the administering organizations publish some results themselves, part of the value of these large-scale, repeated surveys is their ability to provide data to other researchers for further analysis. For example, the National Campaign to Prevent Teen and Unplanned Pregnancy draws on the National Survey of Family Growth (NSFG), discussed later, in noting that almost half of female teens who refrained from sexual activity did so because of religious beliefs.[36] More often, university and government researchers produce peer-reviewed research based on complex analyses of the resulting data.

Each study results in a lengthy bibliography of publications, as well as the baseline statistics.

The YRBSS is a national, longitudinal study that discerns the rates at which U.S. students in grades nine through twelve engage in activities associated with poor health and life outcomes. Sexual activity, now encompassing HIV testing, is one of six areas surveyed through this instrument, but it includes topics like obesity as well. The 2015 YRBSS survey confirmed that recent years have seen decreases in adolescent sexual activity, with slightly more than 40 percent of high-school-aged respondents having had sex at least once, one-third being sexually active beyond an initial encounter, and one-fifth of these teens having made decisions about sex under the influence of drugs or alcohol. The most recent data reveal that fewer than 4 percent of teens in ninth through twelfth grades report their first sexual activity occurred before age thirteen, a decrease from 10 percent in 1991.[37]

These figures are national averages, and state-level analysis indicates that particular communities and constituencies may differ from the big picture. For example, as many as 50 percent of teens in states including Alabama and Wyoming had ever had sex, whereas the rates in Alaska, California, and New York were 30–35 percent.[38] Elsewhere, researchers show variations in teen pregnancy rates within the same city.[39] These contrasts show how the choices of teens in a librarian's own community may vary from national norms, as well as disputing stereotypes about the behaviors of urban versus rural teens.

Age and ethnicity are also analyzed to differentiate results further, and researchers note that results shift from year to year. One article published by the Guttmacher Institute underscored this, noting that while YRBSS data show while the number of high school students reporting sexual activity before age thirteen declined in the last years of the twentieth century, figures increased between 2001 and 2003 but have since declined again. Also significant, according to these authors, is the fact that minority youth were far more likely than their white peers to have had sex prior to age thirteen and to continue their sexual activity.[40] To understand teens and respond to actual information needs with contemporary resources, librarians must monitor the available information on teen sexual activity for its nuances as well as its averages.

Another national longitudinal survey is the National Longitudinal Study of Adolescent to Adult Health (Add Health). The administrators of this grant-funded survey describe it as the "largest, most comprehensive longitudinal survey of adolescents ever undertaken."[41] Launched in 1994, a series of five subsequent questionnaires have gathered data, with the most recent survey taking place in 2016. This study has sought to establish, through research on teens and their parents, the prevalence of early sexual activity, as well as assess attitudes and behaviors associated with good, long-term outcomes. Researchers have endeavored to ensure a nationally representative sample of diverse populations, accounting for ethnicity, age, school size, and urban and rural environments.[42] Data analysis is extensive and ongoing, carried out by individual researchers rather than a government agency, but findings echo some YRBSS conclusions. For example, Add Health surveys indicate that some groups of young people are more likely than others to begin having sex at earlier ages. Rural environments, Southern states, public assistance/welfare, and African-American ethnicity were most strongly associated with younger sexual activity. These findings may represent, for libraries, signals of need for reproductive health information that might be met through strategic collection development or community-based partnerships.

A third survey, undertaken by the National Center for Health Statistics (NCHS) at intervals beginning in 1973, is the NSFG. Created by NCHS, which is part of the U.S. Department of Health and Human Services, the survey includes adults and teens in its examination of attitudes and actions related to issues of reproductive health. There is some variation in questions asked each time the survey is administered, with some questions added and others dropped. The results are designed to help government offices understand and respond to "choices about school, work, and having a family," including access to child care and birth control.[43]

Questions ask about personal choices and beliefs, such as whether mothers should work and whether sex between unmarried individuals and same-sex couples is acceptable. In this, the survey offers a reality check on media coverage of casual sex (only a small minority of young adults describe this as the context in which they've had sex) as well as indications of how teens may respond to contemporary debates about sexual identity (the vast majority of survey respondents agreed, in the language of the survey, that "any sexual act between two consenting adults is all right").[44] One survey asked whether teens were interested in preventing pregnancy (most but not all were, according to 2002 data), if teens younger than eighteen intended to get pregnant (12 percent), and what methods of birth control teens used most often (condoms, with increases in reported usage of other means as well).[45]

These statistical reports on teens and sex document how behaviors change over time. The combination of funding, research expertise, and other resources makes it possible to conduct repeated or ongoing assessments that reflect the national population. This, in turn, allows researchers to outline trends and estimate the scope of suspected problems. These data, however, have limits. Most of the questionnaires used do not inquire about homosexuality, for example, and not all of the instruments look at consent, values, attitudes, or protective factors. To gain information about other aspects of adolescent sexual and reproductive health, librarians can turn to reports issued by organizations like the Henry J. Kaiser Family Foundation, the National Campaign to Prevent Teen and Unplanned Pregnancy, the Urban Institute, and the Guttmacher Institute.

These organizations were among those that made efforts to understand the reality behind public attention to teens and oral sex. For more than ten years, media attention to the role of oral sex in teens' lives has endured. The Urban Institute released a 1995 report on adolescent male sexuality that is often cited as offering the first indications that teens engaged in oral sex. Later, in 2003, the *Washington Post* ran a story claiming oral sex was a newly normal feature of casual sex among teens.[46] Subsequently, other news outlets took up the story, interviewing teens who said they perceived oral sex as a means of preserving their virginity.[47] Because the data behind the news stories were local and anecdotal, and the initial study pertained to male teens only, some of the aforementioned organizations proceeded to broader scientific examination of adolescents' knowledge and attitudes about specific sexual practices. In 2005, then-named National Campaign to Prevent Teen Pregnancy ("and Unplanned" was added later) made the following assessment: "More than half of teens have had oral sex and it is now more likely that a teen has had oral sex than it is that he/she has had sexual intercourse. Almost all of those who have had sexual intercourse have had oral sex (although we do not know the actual sequence of behavior). Moreover, about one in four teens who have *not* had sexual intercourse have had oral sex."[48] Recent studies confirm these trends.

These associations are responsible for many contemporary reports on teen sexuality. Their conclusions sometimes offer further reasons for concern about teens' romantic choices, with attention to the prevalence of violence in intimate relationships (approximately 10 percent to as many as one-third of middle- and high-school-age teens have experienced some sort of ill treatment by a partner), age disparities between sexual partners, and the like.[49] Still other sources of information about adolescence indicate that the "young adult population is one of the subgroups in which the incidence of newly diagnosed [HIV] infection continues to grow quietly."[50] As well as healthy relationships, teens can find themselves in the midst of difficult and disturbing ones. The experts who urge caution regarding teens and sex aren't concerned about a couple like the one at the center of *Why We Broke Up*, or even a less fantastic version of Simon and *Baz in Carry On*; it's these darker and less well-recognized aspects of what can go wrong that generate caution.

Sexual Identity: Subject Guides and Reading Lists

Books like *Rainbow Boys* include contact numbers and URLs for entities that will provide support to LGBTQ teens, and a number of libraries around the nation give specific attention to sexual identity as an area of inquiry and collection development. Among them is the

James C. Hormel LGBTQIA Center at the San Francisco Public Library, which recently celebrated its twentieth anniversary. It and other libraries provide a "gateway to . . . broader collections documenting lesbian, gay, bisexual, transgender, queer, questioning, intersex and allies' history and culture."[51] A selection of additional library pages that can provide reading lists, programming ideas, search terms, and digital resources are listed below.

LGBT@NYC at www.nypl.org/voices/blogs/blog-channels/lgbt/

This blog is designed, as its brief description indicates, to connect "you with the LGBT collections, programs, and expertise that The New York Public Library has to offer." It is arranged in reverse chronological order and lists recent posts by librarians from different divisions within NYPL, offering news about literary awards and more. Of specific interest is a link to the library's digital collections that speak about gay rights, which, the finding aid notes, were collaboratively archived with regional activists. The digital collections contain images of activists, protest literature, and more.

"LGBTQIA Services," Los Angeles Public Library at www.lapl.org/lgbt

This extensive library site includes material specifically for young adults. There are bibliographies that list fiction and nonfiction titles for teens that tell the stories of gay, lesbian, and questioning individuals. Local library events and resources are a focus, but there is still much information here that could support inquiry about sexual identity.

LGBTQI: Subject Guide, Yale University Library at http://guides. library.yale.edu/c.php?g=295883&p=1972807

By using tabs near the top of the page, librarians and library users will find guidance about searching for information and ideas that pertain to varied aspects of sexual identity. This university library page relies on Library of Congress subject headings and emphasizes resources found at Yale; however, it is an eye-opening tool for inquiry regardless. This page identifies new books on gay issues, provides an extensive list of subject headings, and suggests databases and other publications that focus on issues related to sexual identity. While not all links on this site can be used by non-Yale-affiliated individuals and other, Open Web links are no longer operational, it is potentially useful as a collection development resource and in highlighting avenues for information seeking.

Rainbow Book List, Gay, Lesbian, Bisexual, and Transgender Round
Table, ALA at http://glbtrt.ala.org/rainbowbooks/

> Among the endeavors of the ALA round table that gives attention to
> LGBTQ issues is the Rainbow List, which is described as "bibliography
> of books with significant gay, lesbian, bisexual, transgender, or queer/
> questioning content, and which are aimed at youth, birth through age
> 18." The annual list includes notations of particularly recommended
> titles, and works released by small, independent presses are scru-
> tinized for relevance. There is also a separate Stonewall Book Award—
> Mike Morgan and Larry Romans Children's and Young Adult Literature
> Award given by the round table. ■

LIBRARY MATERIALS AND
LIBRARY-ORIENTED RESEARCH

Among professions working with youth, librarians are distinctive
in accepting teens' independent decision making. Core professional
values concerning individuals' freedom of access to information
and fostering young people's development on their own terms have
created an environment that sees teens as adults. *Individuation,* or
separation from parents and family, is a key aspect of adolescence
that youth services librarians now strongly support. We respect teens
as individuals rather than seeing them as children whose parents still
guide them. This stance has been emblematic of the seriousness of
our commitment to young people. It means, too, that we may find
ourselves at odds with others whose interest in young people arises
from different ethical or philosophical orientations.

One way this difference plays out is in complaints about YA
collections. Many libraries hold materials that provide sexual and
reproductive health information to younger readers, and challenges
to books that depict sex as a normal part of the adolescent experience
are almost as routine as the decision to include those titles in our
collections. In any given year, a glance at ALA's Frequently Challenged
Books list reveals a preponderance of titles for teens and children,
accompanied by public concerns that the books are sexually explicit

and "unsuited for age group."[52] Also normal is the publicity that accompanies these challenges, whether it's the 2004 decision of an Arizona teacher-librarian to remove *Deal with It! A Whole New Approach to Your Body, Brain, and Life as a Gurl* from three high school libraries or the 2016 Kentucky educator's efforts to maintain her students' access to *Looking for Alaska*.[53]

Both nonfiction and fiction materials about sexual health foster teens' understanding of sexual and reproductive health issues, according to researchers who indicated the potential for fiction to serve an informative role for teens.[54] From time to time these materials provoke passionate argument, as advocates insist young people's unfettered access to information about sex is perfectly normal, while challengers raise concerns about the appropriateness of content. These competing contentions reflect sincere convictions about who teens are and meeting their reading and information needs appropriately for their different identities. Those needs should be met holistically and inclusively.

Much YA fiction, whether now-classic titles like *Forever* and Alex Sanchez's *Rainbow Boys* or newer titles, feature teen characters who are assertive and informed in their decisions to become sexually active. Authors including Blume and Sanchez argue that young adults have a right to see sexuality depicted in contexts that accept the decisions teens make about life and love. As advocates for young people, they and other authors accept and depict sex as a normal part of adolescence. They give us young adult characters who live happy, well-adjusted lives that include sex.

There are also books for young adults that observe teen protagonists moving from uncertainty and tension to resolution as their ideas about sexuality mature, whether they choose to become sexually active or not. I was disappointed the year I wanted to assign the wittily told story of adolescent love in *Stoner and Spaz,* in which Ben's self-confidence blossoms once Colleen teaches him how attractive he is, demanding that he look beyond the disability that anchors his self-concept, only to learn the book was out of print. Common Sense Media's characterization of the title as an "edgy, sardonic book" that is "OK for mature readers" seems simultaneously apt and out of sync with the way Ben's character becomes stronger and more tender through his relationship with Colleen.[55] Common Sense Media, though intended to give parents a quick guide to whether to allow their children to view or read particular material, is among the websites where librarians can find teens' media reviews. Their comments on Rainbow Rowell's *Fangirl* applaud Cath's virginity but often cringe a bit about profanity on the page. I love the way these younger readers, who recommend the novel for those twelve and up, are unabashedly enthusiastic about it, advising others not to let its 475-page heft "scare you."[56] The unconsummated love story left them wanting more, not fewer, pages.

Much popular debate about teens' sexuality concerns tensions between innocence and experience. While many prominent titles that fill the shelves of our young adult sections show teens making their own decisions about sex, many people question whether teens are in fact able to do so and focus on negative outcomes resulting from teen sexuality. Among parents and the general public, there is considerable disagreement about whether teens are capable, critical decision makers or potential victims of either menacing individuals or of media promoting youth sexuality. Some fear that the teens on the pages of challenged books may have their counterparts in the real world, minus the happy endings.

These discussions perceived potential for Internet activity to endanger young people, and libraries' E-rate funding became linked to their willingness to filter Web content. These topics have their roots in concerns voiced during the first years of this century. In 2006 media reports about provocative teen pages on MySpace prompted Republican members of Congress to require libraries and schools to restrict teen access to this and other social-networking sites. The bill, arguably an extension of the Children's Internet Protection Act enacted in 2001 and updated again in 2011, was promoted as the Deleting Online Predators Act, or DOPA. Its aim was to prevent teens and tweens who interact online from becoming the victims of sex offenders.[57] The provisions of the legislation are still in effect, requiring funded libraries that serve young people to create and enforce usage policies that address "inappropriate matter on the Internet," person-to-person online communication, and "unlawful activities by minors online."[58] While ALA has, in documents like "Fencing Out Knowledge: Impacts of the Children's Internet Protection Act 10 Years Later," insisted that these measures impinge on teens' First Amendment freedoms and restrict the actions of young people who do not have Internet access at home more than others, libraries' Internet filters have become increasingly normal in professional practice.[59]

E-rate-derived restrictions are not the only result national legislation intended to manage teen sexuality. The Teach Safe Relationships Act of 2015 responded to increasing attention to sexual assault and soi-disant shaming by mandating that schools include information about respectful, appropriate conduct in their sex education curricula. Experts have praised the initiative for its interest in securing teens' dignity and well-being, while expressing concern that it aligns with other policies and initiatives that respond to teen sexuality with other approaches, abstinence-until-marriage and sex-as-risk.[60] Urban Institute researchers characterize these responses to teen sexuality as failures in reducing teen pregnancy, rates of sexually transmitted infection (STI), and related concerns. They observe, "Focusing exclusively on abstinence and risk downplays and stigmatizes developmentally appropriate desires youth feel as they mature emotionally and sexually, failing to give teens the tools and context they need to negotiate safe and healthy relationships."[61] Those tools, the research says, include informed conversations about difficult subjects like violence in intimate relationships and other threats to teens' well-being that can accrue in that context. They urge public support for those aims, writing, "Equipping youth (and the families and communities that surround and protect them) with the knowledge and tools they need to support healthy sexual development and relationships—and their related positive outcomes—will get us even further."[62] To me, it is interesting to observe that these writers see family and community as people who help teens become their best selves, rather than entities with the power to prevent it.

There are numerous studies indicating that teens listen to their parents when it comes to sensitive subjects like sex. While there are unsupportive parents and those with unrealistic or unfair notions about teens' behavior, most research has shown repeatedly that the majority of young people do give some credence to their parents' advice. Parents can be assets as teens navigate complex relationships and media messages about sexuality, even if teens do not openly acknowledge their influence.

The library literature has yet to keep pace with the knowledge other fields are developing about teens and sex. While there are a number of essays that explore the topic, often many publications lack a sample size that would allow us to extend the conclusions from the locale under evaluation to our own communities. The more-reliable studies focus on librarians and library resources, rather than teens, and how librarians think about their responsibilities regarding access to sexual and reproductive health information. Those who serve teens sometimes see themselves as creating space for teens to explore sensitive issues or as protecting their interest in controversial content when others might object. For example, one survey about YA web pages highlighted the views of librarians who believed their role in identifying online sources for youth was to call attention to material that would challenge others' values. "I try to broaden their horizons," one librarian said, while another stated, "Our community is very conservative so I think it's important that teen 'issues' be addressed on the YA site."[63] In other words, these librarians approached the sensitive matter of teens' development by defying community mores as they understood them.

Yet there is a difference between creating a balanced collection and functioning as a provocateur. It should be possible to support the needs of genuinely endangered teens, those who lack caring families or guardians, without assuming that every parent-child relationship is fraught with unusual trouble. While the goals of the librarians in the study were congruent with aims of unfettered access to information, we can also consider what we know about good outcomes for young people when providing information about sexual and reproductive health. This aim demands awareness of public health and medical research that indicates there are benefits to abstinence and to connecting messages about sex with parents' moral perspectives. Although it has not been repeated to see if the sentiment holds true fifteen years later, a much-cited 2003 report found that many young, sexually active teens acknowledged wishing they had waited.[64] We need to be true to our belief in young people's rights to inquiry while recognizing that our library resources will be one part of an information ecology they use to respond to information and recreational needs. We need to consider how to collect multiple kinds of resources, given credible research showing that teens are better served by information about reproductive health that expresses values and concerns for their long-term well-being.

Reviewing our collections for how they address sexual and reproductive health information is important. Gross, Goldsmith, and Carruth observe in their *Library Quarterly* article "What Do Young Adult Novels Say about HIV/AIDS? A Second Look" that while HIV/AIDS was seldom meaningfully or effectively addressed in young adult novels published between 1981 and 1994, the titles that followed are often stronger in this regard. The authors note that the "trend toward providing more specific, usable, and personally relevant information to readers is important. It makes these works better vehicles for providing HIV/AIDS education and better sources for modeling behavior in actual contexts that readers might find themselves navigating."[65] Librarians looking for a list of potentially valuable titles will find it in an appendix to this *Library Quarterly* article. Information is also available online, with the CDC consulting with teens to create sexual health information pages for them.[66]

Other professions serving youth believe that information can make a difference in helping teens make appropriate choices about sexual and reproductive health, and they suggest that connections between the teen and the community also matter to teens' well-being. Adolescents' choices about sex are associated with where a teen lives and his socioeconomic status.[67] Further, there is increasing evidence that teens lack adequate information about protecting their sexual health, sometimes believing they possess facts, some of which are simply untrue. One researcher draws attention to the impact of a cultural double standard that encourages young women's erotic dress and flirtation while disapproving of their pursuit of sexual pleasure. Contemporary, interdisciplinary research suggests that teens' sexuality emerges in the midst of broader cultural contexts, not all of which work in teens' favor. These findings represent reasons that librarians should become versed in reliable research on teen sexuality.

Given competing depictions of youth sexuality, librarians who serve young people need to recognize the difference between authoritatively delivered opinion and genuine authority in this area. Additionally, it is useful to be aware of variations—what takes place in different regions, the findings for specific age ranges, and so on—from the national averages provided about teen sexual activity. While teen sexuality has not been a mainstay of LIS research, it is a significant topic in other fields, including public health and medicine. The findings of these researchers can help youth services librarians understand their younger patrons, especially as researchers and practitioners evaluate advances, as is ongoing for "medications which suppress the body's production of estrogen or testosterone, [and] essentially pause the changes that would occur during puberty," a new option for transgender youth.[68] Other public agencies are making efforts to promote teens' healthy development, and librarians interested in partnering with these programs should have some background on teen sexuality from other professional perspectives.

Public health researchers are interested in these issues not because of concerns about teens growing up too fast, but because there are demonstrable negative health and life outcomes when teens become sexually active at an early age. Risk has been a significant concept in the way teen sexual activity is evaluated and understood in the health professions. In those fields, *risk* refers not only to the possibility of poor health but also to barriers to an individual's ability to get an education or earn a living.[69] Risks teens encounter through sexual activity are outlined on a CDC web page that explains that more than 40 percent of teens who have had sex recently did not use condoms and less than 25 percent of sexually active teens have had an HIV test.[70]

Increasingly, though, researchers and policy makers are thinking about teen health less in terms of preventing risk or harm and more in terms of supporting positive development. Still, the risk as a dimension of young people's sexuality hasn't gone away, in part because teens who engage in one kind of risky behavior are more likely to experience other threats to health and well-being.[71] Sexual activity carries greater risks for younger adolescents, in part because those who are fifteen years of age and younger have higher rates of infection and pregnancy.[72] In this context, adolescent sexuality is more than a matter of personal choices or cultural values about premarital sex. It is among the behaviors or conditions that health professionals address through information and counseling in support of outcomes with personal and public benefits.[73] These facts are why the American Academy of Pediatrics advises doctors to counsel adolescents to delay sexual activity until closer to adulthood.[74] Librarians do not need to voice this kind of message, only to include it among the perspectives on sex represented in their collections.

There are still other significant aspects of recent nongovernmental research on adolescent sexuality. Multiple researchers are finding that some young people who engage in oral sex think of themselves as abstinent. This is important not because of how it plays out in polls or surveys but because these teens don't protect themselves from the risk of STIs. These findings reveal information deficits that effectively discourage adolescents from seeking information about safe sex practices. As National Campaign to Prevent Teen and Unplanned Pregnancy researchers concluded, "Too many teens view oral sex as safe."[75] Of particular concern in recent years is the tendency of gay and lesbian teens to eschew protection because they are unconcerned with birth control.

Other investigations of teens' attitudes toward sex have been conducted. One notable effort to investigate news reports about patterns of casual sex was undertaken by Child Trends in 2003 and updated later. This survey of U.S. teens found that the vast majority of young people described their first sexual encounter as part of a romantic relationship. Still, problems were evident in teens' descriptions of their first sexual relationships, with significant numbers of girls fourteen years of age and younger reporting partners two or more years older than themselves and 21 percent of those surveyed saying they never used contraception during the length of the relationship. Also of concern was the incidence of intimate-partner violence, which occurred in 25 percent of those surveyed, with higher figures among

Hispanic teens. Researchers also noted that 80 percent of these first intimate relationships lasted, on average, six months.[76] This report, which shows broad patterns that hold true in subsequent research, is interesting because it depends on young people's perceptions of their own behavior. It doesn't dismiss teens' rose-colored evaluations of their sexual relationships while drawing attention to the risks inherent in these perspectives.

Another study of teens' perceptions of their sexuality was conducted by Deborah L. Tolman. Concerned by a continuing double standard for sexual activity (a problem that researchers and activists in the United States and abroad began decrying at the turn of the previous century), Tolman interviewed young women about what their sexual experiences meant to them. How did these young women perceive their sexual desires in a culture that sent them mixed messages about female sexuality? There is no single answer, Tolman found, but she writes, "At a time when we are told there is a 'war on boys' and that girls are just fine, the voices of girls in this study sound a different note, reminding us that being a girl, living comfortably in a girl's body, is neither easy nor especially safe."[77] Tolman talks about the value of conversations among women to make teen girls feel empowered and to enable them to make healthy choices. She advocates for sexuality education and for girls' right to make choices about their bodies and their feelings. Instead of statistics, she offers narratives that depict girls' uncertainties, issues, and information needs.

Tolman is one researcher among many who raise questions about how the media influence teens' thinking about sexuality. The connections between what teens see and hear via television or the movies and what they do in their own lives is complex. For years, communications researchers have criticized what has become known as the magic-bullet effect—the idea that a message is uttered and the receiver responds exactly as intended. Yet some recent research is beginning to suggest that there may indeed be relationships between teens' actions and the sexualized images so often found on-screen. These findings are nascent, and it has been observed that, as yet, no research accounts for the entirety of teens' media consumption, particularly their intense involvement with music.[78] A limited amount of research indicates that there are correlations between teens' viewing habits and their sexual activity. As researchers bluntly stated, "watching sex on TV predicts and may hasten adolescent sexual initiation."[79] It should be noted, though, that researchers found differences by racial groups, with the predictive factor more demonstrable for white teens than for African-Americans. The RAND Corporation published survey data indicating that aggressively sexual lyrics in contemporary popular music are associated with earlier initiation of sexual activity.[80] More recently, other researchers who conducted a focus group with teens found that media influenced teens' talk about relationships, offering them a vocabulary for their experiences: "When naming and defining relationships, young teens were more likely to refer to song lyrics, television commercials, and other aspects of pop culture."[81] These kinds of conclusions factor into medical associations' advice that physicians provide assessment and counseling regarding young people's media consumption.

At the same time that popular appeal has become an accepted facet of collection development and library promotion, other fields are beginning to express concerns about the impact that some material—generally, broadcast media—has on young people's sexual health. Librarians can respond to young people's professed interest in popular media while considering expert opinion by ensuring balanced, diverse content in their collections.

CONCLUSION

What do the numbers and research findings about teen sexuality mean for librarians? Where do such findings lead us as we develop collections for young adults? Are there ideas for programming or other services that emerge from the findings?

One idea, perhaps the most obvious, is that research offers librarians a way of understanding teens. Beyond urban legends and anecdotes, the numbers indicate something about what it means to be a sexually active U.S. teenager or even a teen in the midst of a youth culture where sexuality is a prevalent concern. The available figures show that teens' experiences of sexuality are far from uniform. Statistics differentiate between teens who have had sex but are no longer sexually active, those who have continued to have a sexual relationship with a single partner, and others who have pursued sexual relationships with multiple partners. It follows that each group will have different information needs and that different sorts of fiction will represent the health and relationship issues they experience. Statistical descriptions of teens' sexual experiences, which don't always mirror what teens say "everyone is doing," offer a big-picture perspective on a sensitive, personal matter that also represents a known area of information seeking by adolescents.

Most research does not direct our actions, but it should encourage us to reflect on our practices. Whether it's news reports about adolescent sexuality or the grapevine in our own communities that spurs our commitment to making reproductive health materials available, we nonetheless need to weigh what we're being told. Scientific findings, in addition to local angles on the big story, should guide our assessment of adolescents' needs for information about sex and their bodies. We sometimes assume that those who advocate chastity act out of misguided nostalgia for an innocent past that may never have existed, yet research indicates that teens benefit from waiting when it comes to sex. Looking for ways to represent this perspective can be a component of providing sexual and reproductive health information for younger teens. Including diverse perspectives, which is a long-advocated means of creating balance in the collection, is valuable in this area too: teens should have access to an array of information that will support and inform their reproductive health choices.

One assessment of sex education programs found that effective means of preventing teen pregnancies and reducing STI were grounded in improving teens' relationships and communication with their parents.[82] This finding does not suggest we should assume parents and teens communicate openly, much less that parents have a right to intervene in their teens' information seeking. It does represent important contextual information about how our professional peers work with teens. If our libraries work with experts interested in decreasing teen childbearing, we should anticipate that those practitioners may expect teens' parents to be part of the conversation.

We need to consider whether making health information available via our teen websites is a strong service option. Research has shown that less than 50 percent of the fourteen- to seventeen-year-olds surveyed had used a library's website, and sizable proportions of other, older individuals said they were unaware their libraries had websites.[83] At the same time, research on censorship has shown that libraries may be targeted for these recommendations.[84] One reality of teens' online information seeking is that they most often look for reproductive health information via search engines rather than online pathfinders. Yet such searches, conducted because of their potential for confidentiality, can be hampered by spelling and unfamiliarity with site-evaluation strategies. Librarians can convey knowledge about credible and appropriate online sites through reference recommendations and other interactions with teens or even the adults in their lives.

In the context of contemporary concerns about young people's sexuality, what should our collections look like? When I discuss a book like *Forever* with my students, they often cite Blume's statement that she wrote it because her daughter wanted to read a book that didn't punish teens for having sex, and they want to talk about the importance of this perspective in the library. Librarians I know who have hosted Alex Sanchez and other writers who deal with sensitive topics talk about teens' enthusiasm for such messages and describe individuals who find tremendous reassurance from such stories. Certainly, many controversial titles speak to young readers and ease their angst about matters they feel unable to discuss in other contexts. My point in this chapter is not to suggest that such books should be removed or that teens should be frightened with threats of disease or unmarried pregnancy that might be borne out by statistics. In fact, research suggests that parental values and communication, not fear-based appeals, deter teens from irresponsible decisions. Librarians serving young adults must consider how to acquire a range of materials that support not only sexual curiosity but also sexual health, not only materials that reinforce teens' idealized or impulsive inclinations but also resources that can ground responsible decision making or dialogue with supportive parents.

When thinking about how library collections support teens' development, consider the messages in materials that deal with sexuality. Does a magazine featuring alluring teen pop stars include advertisements, also known as public service announcements, or PSAs, that encourage sexually active teens to use birth control, for example?[85] Do sexually active fictional characters use birth control? While not every resource must provide a public health message, it's desirable to have some material indicating to teens that there is more to sex than pleasure, particularly given recent studies that suggest many teens do base their expectations and actions on the consequence-free sexuality prevalent in the mass media. LIS educators Kendra Albright and Karen Gavigan worked with South Carolina teens to develop a graphic novel about AIDS that reflects both very real health threats and the tensions of teen life.[86] Librarians should be aware of popular criticism of the resulting publication, considering whether critiques are, essentially, a call for ideal messages and narratives of which adults approve.[87]

We might also consider the implications of including some kinds of popular media in our young adult collections, just as other professions have begun to question whether broadcast sexual images and dialogue have negative impacts on young adults' well-being. Most of this research does not account for popular magazines and music, although it deals with related media such as the videos and other television programs young people watch. Some new research takes on popular music, and the findings there correlate with those for other media.

While librarians have sought to shed their image as stuffy literary purists by collecting popular music and magazines featuring pop stars, researchers have begun to investigate relationships between activities like television viewing and teens' risk-taking behaviors. This work, some of which is in relatively early stages, raises questions about whether media that many teens find appealing are, after all, fully harmless. Increasingly, researchers are identifying the influence of media on youths' perceptions of their bodies and significant personal choices. Librarians seem reluctant to accept the idea that media have negative effects, associating such statements with historical arguments about the threats posed by bad books. There is suspicion that concerns about media's effects could translate into the removal of resources. Yet in fields that acknowledge media have both positive and negative influences, few researchers advocate banning materials. Instead, there is interest in how media achieve effects and how less-desirable consequences can be mitigated.

The dilemma of creating a collection based on perceived patron appeal versus an expert notion of what ought to be there has been debated repeatedly. The history of youth services depicts librarians hoping to attract young people to good literature and decrying the perceived harm of popular fiction and comics with their more adventurous content. Regardless of the importance of avoiding this sort of restrictive, black-and-white thinking, informed practice of our professional responsibilities requires us to appreciate that researchers are looking for ways to understand how the media that teens favor affect their reproductive health. Researchers in cognate fields suggest balancing the ready appeal of, say, *Gossip Girls* series fiction with other titles that provide different messages about body image, risky behaviors, and sexuality.

In collecting material about sexual and reproductive health, we should keep in mind the need to serve patrons with low-level literacy skills. Specialists who study U.S. literacy rates, in tandem with experts who focus on the specific area of health literacy, call attention to the importance of collecting material that clarifies health issues in language that can be understood easily. This presents another challenge for people who select reproductive health materials for young people—finding resources that are easy to read yet don't talk down to their audience.

Increasingly, public health educators discuss the need to guide young people toward healthy and productive adulthood by facilitating their sense of belonging and participation in activities that help them prepare for their futures. Partnerships are one means of working toward these aims, which suggests that librarians are well-positioned to support them. Librarians should seek opportunities to work with others who specialize in adolescent development and join public health professionals in encouraging teens to pursue education and community involvement as part of a broader effort to decrease risks like early sexual initiation.

In contemporary libraries, librarians have refused to act in the place of parents to keep young people from accessing materials that might be considered mature or risqué. We have paid considerable attention to providing nonjudgmental responses to young people's sensitive queries, particularly with regard to sexuality. We've recognized their individuality and the ways their views and experimentation may differ from those of others. Through these acts and more, we've championed teens' rights and interests. While recognizing teens' interests in becoming autonomous individuals who are comfortable with their sexuality, librarians should consider how they can bring the lessons learned by other professionals to support interactions with teens in library settings. We can't emulate health counselors, but we might evaluate strategic ways to make referrals and find other means of connecting teens with professionals able to give advice about health and long-term decisions.

As we serve teens, the following ideas about young people's decisions to become sexually active are important:

> There are good reasons for teens to delay sex. Higher-than-average risks of STIs and pregnancy are among the problems experienced by young teens who don't wait.[88] Many reputable medical associations, including the Society for Adolescent Medicine, recommend making abstinence one component of sex education, which suggests that abstinence should be one part of the information about sexual and reproductive health available in libraries for teens.

> Research indicates that teens are, for the most part, able to make sense of health information that counsels them to abstain but tells them how to protect themselves if they are sexually active. Librarians don't need to fear providing a mixed message through resources that make these statements.

Parents as well as teens need information about adolescent sexual and reproductive health. For example, the medical community has discussed the age at which girls might be vaccinated against human papillomavirus and whether there are benefits to vaccinating boys too. Doctors and public health officials have discussed the value of the vaccine for eleven-year-olds, an age at which girls and boys may be potential users of young adult library services but are not old enough to make their own decisions about medical care. As issues that affect young people's needs for health information develop, materials may be added to parenting collections and other areas of the library that reach adult caregivers.

Sexual and reproductive health should be addressed holistically. Recent studies report that young women fail to understand the connections between diet, exercise, and breast cancer. In this context, supporting teens' sexual and reproductive health means more than providing resources on reproductive biology, contraception, and STIs.

Librarians need to know about their state's laws governing the age at which young people can give consent for medical care. These laws affect young people's ability to obtain health care, including reproductive health services. While research has indicated that most teens do involve their parents in their reproductive health decisions, even when dealing with sensitive and controversial situations like abortion, there may be young people in your community who need to know not only about their options for reproductive health care, but also about their legal right to obtain services.[89]

More reproductive health information, including material on birth control and STIs, is prepared for adolescent girls than for adolescent boys. Experts agree, though, that getting appropriate information to male teens is a much-needed part of ensuring good health. Seeking sources that are authoritative and able to communicate with young men should be a priority in collection development.

It has been observed that appropriate, nondiscriminatory material for teens who are not heterosexual is an important but often overlooked aspect of meeting information needs. Given statistics on the disproportionate representation of LGBTQ teens among the homeless population, ready access to information about local or regional support services is vital to serving teens, as is health information.

The basics, in terms of both content and language, should not be overlooked. Teens' confidence in their reproductive health knowledge sometimes exceeds its accuracy, and researchers are recognizing that large segments of the U.S. population require information resources that assume only the most basic literacy levels. These findings mean that regardless of teens' perceived sexual sophistication, there is a little-acknowledged need for foundational information that can be understood by those whose reading level lags behind their grade level.

Despite the mythic power of teen hormones, teen sexual behavior is influenced by many factors, including parental involvement and media messages. New research is providing more information about these interactions, offering the proverbial food for thought about the merits of some popular materials. We want to believe books have powerful positive effects, and that power can be unpredictable. As John Berry once wrote, "If words don't incite action, I'm in the wrong line of work. . . . If they don't motivate people to act, antisocially or otherwise, then our First Amendment is of little value and less importance. This is a tough contradiction for those of us who must argue the case against censorship. . . . We can't support free expression by saying it won't do any harm. It is obvious that action triggered by words and pictures can do harm and often does."[90] No one in our profession advocates getting rid of books or other media that sanction teen sex; instead, the important thing, researchers say, is to look for ways to balance those messages with others that give attention to other aspects of identity and adulthood.

Statistics say teen sex is declining, but there's more to this story. The numbers vary by state, age, and ethnicity. Plus, while recent numbers represent improvements, the United States still ranks among the developed nations with the highest rates of teen pregnancy. These facts suggest that more is required to help teens make choices in their own best interests.

Anecdotes can be compelling, but evidence-based research about sexual health is more important to improving outcomes for young people. Look for ways to confirm contentions about teen sexuality using research by NGOs or with local public health officials, for example, to confirm that there's a trend or an information need that should be reflected in the collection. One resource that can provide data is Key Information about U.S. States (https://thena tionalcampaign.org/resource/key-information-about-us -states), a searchable resource created by the National Campaign to Prevent Teen and Unplanned Pregnancy, to offer ready access to statistics, reproductive health grants, and related matters.

Librarians negotiate many tensions as they serve young people. Few aspects of library service are more controversial than efforts to inform and to support adolescents' interests in their developing sexuality, whether teens are gay or straight; whether the materials are factual or fiction; whether the resources are on library shelves or the World Wide Web. Possessing an informed and nuanced perspective on teen sexuality is a necessary step in our efforts to communicate with teens and the rest of the community about the reasons for including resources about sensitive issues in our collections. By grounding decisions about providing sexual and reproductive health information in empirical, interdisciplinary research, we are better able to select useful and appropriate information as well as make strategic decisions about how we provide access to these resources. This does not ask us to censor recreational materials or reduce access to reproductive health information in libraries. It is a call to ensure that we provide teens with the best possible materials to address subjects that they may be hesitant to ask for, supplementing our professional values with other professions' research intended to help teens as they mature. That knowledge, most of which highlights the importance of teens' ability to get answers to their health questions, can enhance our choices and expand our sense of what is possible in an area of the collection that draws a disproportionate amount of public scrutiny.

FOR FURTHER READING

Jardin, Xeni. "How to Talk about Caitlyn Jenner: A Guide to Speaking and Writing about Transgender People." *Boing Boing,* June 1, 2015. http://boingboing.net/2015/06/01/how-to-talk -about-caitlyn-jenn.html.

> If you are trying to navigate the complex array of nouns and pronouns that describe sexual identity, this online guide, developed in consultation with GLAAD, an advocacy organization that promotes positive public conversations about LGBTQ issues, may help. It not only indicates what terms might give offense, it also explains why certain language is regarded as problematic and why the alternatives are preferable.

The National Campaign to Prevent Teen and Unplanned Pregnancy. "Latino Community." https://thenationalcampaign .org/featured-topics/latino-community/.

> Citing data showing that the proportion of Latina teens who become pregnant is higher than in other U.S. ethnic groups, this

site provides a variety of messages intended to help reverse this trend. It contains resources in English and in Spanish, including videos and other materials for teens, like the downloadable pamphlet, "Thinking About Our Future." The organization produces an array of resources that aim to speak to teens of varied backgrounds as well as the adults who interact with them.

Orenstein, Peggy. *Girls and Sex: Navigating the Complicated New Landscape*. New York: HarperCollins, 2016.

Orenstein, a mother and author, interviewed young women about their sexual experiences and attitudes. She describes unwanted attention, both verbal and physical, as well as the cultural and corporate factors she sees as detrimental to young women's self-concepts and others' respect. While a *New York Times* review observes that Orenstein is of a different generation than her subjects, who are not uniformly troubled by the experiences (or clothing) that disconcert her, Orenstein herself cites a British feminist who dismisses controversial, potentially self-demeaning choices enacted only by women and not by men as something other than activism or revolution (ch. 2). The stories of young women's experiences come across as alternately harrowing and confused, particularly when contextualized by explicit accounts of media that reduce women to the status of not-particularly-well-regarded objects. The book represents a detailed portrait of the worst of how sex and sexuality can be used to degrade and attack young women, whether lesbian or straight.

Ryan, Suzanne, Jennifer Manlove, and Kerry Franzetta. "The First Time: Characteristics of Teens' First Sexual Relationships." *Child Trends Research Brief* 2003-16, August 2003. www.childtrends.org/wp-content/uploads/2003/08/First-Time.pdf.

The bottom line of this analysis is in decided contrast with news reports about young people's casual sexual relationships: "The majority of teens' first sexual relationships were with a romantic partner." Other findings, however, revealed significant age differences between partners, rates of nonuse of contraception, and violence or verbal abuse in a significant minority of teen relationships.

Schwartz, John. *Oddly Normal: One Family's Struggle to Help Their Teenage Son Come to Terms with His Sexuality.* New York: Gotham, 2012.

> This parental narrative debuted to positive, empathetic reviews that found a father's account of attempting to create a supportive environment for his gay, teenage son convincing and, at times, even funny. It is not a simple story, beginning with the son's attempted suicide and including the acknowledgment of other mental health issues clouding the picture. Research supports and supplements the narrative, which offers a window into the life and struggles of one teen and his family.

Selznick, Brian. "'Love Is a Dangerous Angel': Thoughts on Queerness and Family in Children's Books." *Children and Libraries* 13, no. 4 (Winter 2015): 3–12.

> Selznick's Arbuthnot lecture, the text of which subsequently appeared in the Association for Library Service to Children (ALSC) magazine, cited above, discusses many topics that concern YAs and YA librarians. Beyond his broadly declared topic of family, Selznick discusses his developing identity, beginning with his years in middle school, reading the iconic YA novel, *Weetzie Bat,* David Levithan's *Boy Meets Boy,* and the Bible. For YA librarians, it's a must-read account of one teen's understanding of his gay identity and the sometimes loving and sometimes fraught family conversations that LGBTQ teens experience.

Sexual Health of Adolescents and Young Adults in the United States. Menlo Park, CA: Henry J. Kaiser Family Foundation, 2014. http://kff.org/womens-health-policy/fact-sheet/sexual-health-of-adolescents-and-young-adults-in-the-united-states.

> This study uses national survey data to describe trends in contemporary sexual relationships among teens and young adults. Issues ranging from sexual activity, number of partners, use of birth control, rape, and sexting are accounted for statistically. Access to reproductive health services is also assessed. The strengths and limits of teens' knowledge about STIs and birth control are described.

"20 Mighty Girl Books for Tweens & Teens About Healthy Relationships." *A Mighty Girl Blog,* February 22, 2016. www.amightygirl.com/blog?p=11338.

This annotated bibliography of YA novels whose plots turn on romantic relationships was developed for Dating Violence Awareness Month. It features novels, from Nicola Yoon's *Everything, Everything* to Nancy Garden's *Annie on My Mind,* and nonfiction for teens and parents about problems in relationships.

NOTES

1. The original version of this chapter reflected, in part, research first published in my essay, "Research Directions for Understanding and Responding to Young Adult Sexual and Reproductive Health Information Needs," in *Youth Information Seeking Behavior: Theories, Models, and Issues,* vol. 2, ed. Mary K. Chelton and Colleen Cool (Lanham, MD: Scarecrow Press, 2007). Some of that content remains in this edition as well.

2. Lina Guzman et al., "Telling It Like It Is: Teen Perspectives on Romantic Relationships," *Child Trends Research Brief* 2009–44 (October 2009), 1, www.childtrends.org/publications/telling-it-like-it-is-teen-perspectives-on-romantic-relationships; Gu Li and Melissa Hines, "In Search of Emerging Same Sex Sexuality: Romantic Attractions at Age 13," *Archives of Sexual Behavior* 45, no. 7 (October 2016): 1839–49, doi:10.1007/s10508-016-0726-2.

3. Elizabeth Wildsmith et al., "The Dynamics in Young Adult Romantic Relationships: Important for Success in Love—and in Life," *Child Trends Research Brief* 2013–37 (December 2013), www.childtrends.org/wp-content/uploads/2013/12/2013-37DynamicsYoungAdultRomanticRelationships1.pdf.

4. "Adolescent Sexuality," Sexuality Information and Education Council of the United States, www.siecus.org/index.cfm?fuseaction=Page.ViewPage&pageId=620.

5. NowThis, "President Obama Hosted a Reception for LGBT Pride Month," video, June 9, 2016, www.facebook.com/NowThisNews/videos/1080921775331279; Corinne Segal, "Oregon Court Rules That 'Nonbinary' Is a Legal Gender," *PBS NewsHour,* June 11, 2016, www.pbs.org/newshour/rundown/oregon-court-rules-that-nonbinary-is-a-legal-gender.

6. Faith Karimi and Catherine E. Soichet, "High School Grad, Dancer, Accountant Among Orlando Shooting Victims," CNN, June 16, 2016, www.cnn.com/2016/06/13/us/orlando-victims-profiles.

7. Ariel Zambelich and Cassi Alexandra, "Months After Pulse Shooting, 'There Is a Wound on the Entire Community,'" National Public Radio, December 13, 2016, www.npr.org/2016/12/13/503867756/months-after -pulse-shooting-there-is-a-wound-on-the-entire-community.

8. Andrew Marszal, "Transgender Activist Dies After Being 'Denied Treatment' for Gun Wounds in Pakistan Hospital," *The Telegraph*, May 25, 2016, www.telegraph.co.uk/news/2016/05/25/transgender-activist -dies-after-being-denied-treatment-in-pakist.

9. Claire Landsbaum, "House Republicans Block Vote on LGBT Protections After Orlando Shooting," *New York Magazine*, June 15, 2016, http:// nymag.com/daily/intelligencer/2016/06/house-blocks-vote-on-lgbt -protections.html; Emmarie Huetteman, "G.O.P. Opposition to Gay Rights Provision Derails Spending Bill," *New York Times*, May 26, 2016, www.nytimes.com/2016/05/27/us/politics/house-budget-gay-rights-paul -ryan.html.

10. Department of Justice Office of Public Affairs, "U.S. Departments of Justice and Education Release Joint Guidance to Help Schools Ensure the Civil Rights of Transgender Students," press release, May 13, 2016, www.justice.gov/opa/pr/us-departments-justice-and-education-release -joint-guidance-help-schools-ensure-civil-rights.

11. Julie Hirschfield Davis and Matt Apuzzo, "U.S. Directs Public Schools to Allow Transgender Access to Restrooms," *New York Times*, May 12, 2016, www.nytimes.com/2016/05/13/us/politics/obama-administration -to-issue-decree-on-transgender-access-to-school-restrooms.html?_r=0.

12. Megan Cottrell, "Libraries Create Gender-Neutral Bathrooms," *American Libraries*, October 30, 2015, http://americanlibrariesmagazine.org/2015/ 10/30/libraries-gender-neutral-bathrooms.

13. Darla Miles, "NY Public Library Holds 'Anti-Prom' for LGBT Students," ABC7NY, June 17, 2016, http://abc7ny.com/society/ny-public-library -holds-anti-prom/1391153.

14. "Frequently Challenged Books," American Library Association, 2015, www.ala.org/bbooks/frequentlychallengedbooks; Scott Cousins, "The Practice of Challenging 'Bad' Books," *The Telegraph*, April 16, 2016, http://thetelegraph.com/news/81092/the-practice-if-challenging-bad -books; Vlogbrothers, "On the Banning of Looking for Alaska," YouTube video, April 12, 2016, www.youtube.com/watch?v=69rd-7vEF3s.

15. Vlogbrothers, "I Am Not a Pornographer," YouTube video, January 30, 2008, www.youtube.com/watch?v=fHMPtYvZ8tM.

16. Kristin Pekoll, "Support *Looking for Alaska*," *Intellectual Freedom Blog*, April 27, 2016, www.oif.ala.org/oif/?p=6524.

17. Allison Pond, Gregory Smith, and Scott Clement, "Religion Among the Millennials," Pew Research Center, February 17, 2010, www.pewforum .org/2010/02/17/religion-among-the-millennials.

18. Nerdfighteria Census 2015, www.surveymonkey.com/r/xg96qsh; *Urban Dictionary*, s.v. "cis," www.urbandictionary.com/define.php?term=cis.

19. Michael Schulman, "Generation LGBTQIA," *New York Times*, January 9, 2013, E1, www.nytimes.com/2013/01/10/fashion/generation-lgbtqia .html.

20. Ine Vanwesenbeeck, "More Colors in a Rainbow," *Archives of Sexual Behavior* 45, no. 3 (April 2016): 521–23, doi:10.1007/s10508-015 -0627-9.

21. Li and Hines, "In Search of Emerging Same Sex Sexuality."

22. Schulman, "Generation LGBTQIA."

23. Ibid.

24. Julie Bindel, "Viewpoint: Should Gay Men and Lesbians Be Bracketed Together?" *BBC Magazine*, July 2, 2014, www.bbc.com/news/ magazine-28130472.

25. Ryan Carey-Mahoney, "LGBT-who? Decoding the Ever-Changing Acronym," *Washington Post*, June 10, 2016, www.washingtonpost .com/news/soloish/wp/2016/06/10/lgbt-who-decoding-the-ever -changing-acronym.

26. Alex Gino, *George* (New York: Scholastic Press, 2015).

27. Guzman et al., "Telling It Like It Is," 1.

28. Deborah L. Tolman, "The Lost Children of Rockdale County," *Frontline*, 1999, www.pbs.org/wgbh/pages/frontline/shows/georgia.

29. "YRBSS Frequently Asked Questions," Division of Adolescent and School Health, 2016, www.cdc.gov/healthyyouth/data/yrbs/faq.htm#top5.

30. "2011–2013 NSFG: Public Use Data Files, Codebooks, and Documentation," National Center for Health Statistics, 2016, www.cdc .gov/nchs/nsfg/nsfg_2011_2013_puf.htm.

31. Heather Fish, Jennifer Manlove, and Kristin Anderson Moore, "What Works for Adolescent Sexual and Reproductive Health: Lessons from Experimental Programs and Interventions," *Child Trends Research Brief* 2014–64 (December 2014), www.childtrends.org/?research

-briefs=what-works-for-adolescent-sexual-and-reproductive-health
#sthash.dZ5KG2YO.dpuf.

32. Mindy E. Scott et al., "Characteristics of Young Adult Sexual Relationships: Diverse, Sometimes Violent, Often Loving," *Child Trends Research Brief* 2011–01 (January 2011): 3, www.childtrends .org/wp-content/uploads/2011/01/Child_Trends-2011_01_05_RB _YoungAdultShips.pdf.

33. "Statistics You Should Know About Gay & Transgender Students," PFLAG New York City, 2016, www.pflagnyc.org/safeschools/statistics.

34. Rachel Feltman, "Study: Same Sex Experiences Are on the Rise, and Americans Are Increasingly Chill About It," *Washington Post,* June 1, 2016, www.washingtonpost.com/news/speaking-of-science/wp/2016/ 06/01/study-same-sex-experiences-are-on-the-rise-and-americans-are-increasingly-chill-about-it.

35. Ibid.

36. "Religion and Values," The National Campaign to Prevent Teen and Unplanned Pregnancy, 2016, https://thenationalcampaign.org/featured -topics/religion-and-values.

37. "Trends in the Prevalence of Sexual Behaviors and HIV Testing, National YRBS: 1991–2015," Division of Adolescent and School Health, www.cdc.gov/healthyyouth/data/yrbs/pdf/trends/2015_us_sexual_trend _yrbs.pdf.

38. "YRBSS Results," Division of Adolescent and School Health, 2016, www.cdc.gov/healthyyouth/data/yrbs/results.htm.

39. Jennifer Manlove et al., "Location Matters: Geographic Variation in Teen Childbearing within Washington, D.C.," *Child Trends Research Brief* 2014–58 (November 2014), www.childtrends.org/?research-briefs =location-matters.

40. Lydia O'Donnell et al., "Saving Sex for Later: An Evaluation of a Parent Education Intervention," *Perspectives on Sexual and Reproductive Health* 37, no. 4 (December 2005): 166–73.

41. "About," Add Health: The National Longitudinal Study of Adolescent to Adult Health, www.cpc.unc.edu/projects/addhealth/about.

42. Kathleen Mullan Harris et al., "Study Design," Add Health: The National Longitudinal Study of Adolescent to Adult Health, www.cpc.unc.edu/ projects/addhealth/design.

43. "Welcome NSFG Participants," National Center for Health Statistics, 2014, www.cdc.gov/nchs/nsfg/participant.htm.

44. "Key Statistics from the National Survey of Family Growth," National Center for Health Statistics, 2012, www.cdc.gov/nchs/nsfg/key_statistics .htm.

45. J. C. Abma et al., "Teenagers in the United States: Sexual Activity, Contraceptive Use, and Childbearing, 2002," National Center for Health Statistics, *Vital Health Statistics* 23, no. 24 (2004).

46. Laura Sessions Stepp, "The Buddy System/Sex in High School and College: What's Love Got to Do with It?" *Washington Post,* January 19, 2003.

47. Sharon Jayson, "'Technical Virginity' Becomes Part of Teens' Equation," *USA Today,* October 19, 2005.

48. National Campaign to Prevent Teen Pregnancy, "Teens and Oral Sex," *Putting What Works to Work: Science Says* 17 (September 2005): 5.

49. "Prevalence of Teen Dating Violence," National Institute of Justice, 2016, www.nij.gov/topics/crime/intimate-partner-violence/teen-dating-violence/ pages/prevalence.aspx.

50. Kaiser Foundation, cited in Melissa Gross, Annette Goldsmith, and Debi Carruth, "What Do Young Adult Novels Say about HIV/AIDS? A Second Look," *Library Quarterly* 78, no. 4 (October 2008): 398.

51. "James C. Hormel LGBTQIA Center - 3rd Floor," San Francisco Public Library, 2016, http://sfpl.org/?pg=0200002401.

52. "Frequently Challenged Books," American Library Association, 2016, www.ala.org/bbooks/frequentlychallengedbooks.

53. "Arizona School District Removes Teen-Advice Title," *American Libraries,* October 8, 2004, https://americanlibrariesmagazine.org/ arizona-school-district-removes-teen-advice-title/; Alison Flood, "US Battle Over Banning *Looking for Alaska* Continues in Kentucky," *The Guardian,* April 28, 2016, www.theguardian.com/books/2016/apr/28/ battle-keep-looking-for-alaska-kentucky-school-curriculum-john-green-ya; Lauren Barack, "*Looking for Alaska* Stays in Curriculum in Lebanon, KY," *School Library Journal* blog, May 16, 2016, www.slj.com/2016/05/ censorship/looking-for-alaska-stays-in-curriculum-in-lebanon-kentucky/; Sarah Hoffman, "*Looking for Alaska* Under Fire in Kentucky," *National Coalition Against Censorship Blog,* April 5, 2016, http://ncac.org/blog/ looking-for-alaska-under-fire-in-kentucky.

54. Patricia J. Campbell, *Sex Guides: Books and Films about Sexuality for Young Adults* (New York: Garland, 1986); Melissa Gross, "Library Service to Pregnant Teens: How Can We Help?" *School Library Journal* 43, no. 6 (June 1997): 36–37; Amy Pattee, "The Secret Source: Sexually

Explicit Young Adult Literature as an Information Source," *Young Adult Library Services* 4, no. 2 (Fall 2005): 30–38.

55. Matt Berman, review of *Stoner & Spaz,* by Ron Koertge, Common Sense Media, www.commonsensemedia.org/book-reviews/stoner-spaz#.

56. Sandie Angulo Chen, review of *Fangirl,* by Rainbow Rowell, Common Sense Media, www.commonsensemedia.org/book-reviews/fangirl. See especially 17-year-old OliviaGreen's review titled "Good book for any day!!" October 22, 2014.

57. Declan McCullagh, "Congress Targets Social Network Sites," *ZDNet,* June 29, 2006, www.zdnet.com/article/congress-targets-social-networking -sites.

58. Federal Communications Commission, "Children's Internet Protection Act," 2015, www.fcc.gov/consumers/guides/childrens-internet-protection -act.

59. Kristen R. Batch, "Fencing Out Knowledge: Impacts of the Children's Internet Protection Act 10 Years Later," *American Library Association Policy Brief* 5 (June 2014), http://connect.ala.org/files/cipa_report.pdf.

60. Laudan Y. Aron and Janine M. Zweig, "Teen Sex—Yes, Let's Talk About It," *Urban Wire,* February 12, 2015, www.urban.org/urban-wire/teen -sex-yes-lets-talk-about-it.

61. Ibid.

62. Ibid.

63. Sandra Hughes-Hassell and Erika Thickman Miller, "Public Library Websites for Young Adults: Meeting the Needs of Today's Teens Online," *Library and Information Research* 25, no. 2 (2003): 143–56.

64. *Fourteen and Younger: The Sexual Behavior of Young Adolescents* (Washington, DC: National Campaign to Prevent Teen Pregnancy, 2003).

65. Gross, Goldsmith, and Carruth, "What Do Young Adult Novels Say about HIV/AIDS? A Second Look," *The Library Quarterly* 78, no. 4 (October 2008), 414.

66. "For Teens," Division of Reproductive Health, www.cdc.gov/teenpreg nancy/teens.

67. Priyanka Boghani, "When Transgender Kids Transition, Medical Risks Are Both Known and Unknown," *Frontline,* June 10, 2015. www.pbs .org/wgbh/frontline/article/when-transgender-kids-transition-medical -risks-are-both-known-and-unknown.

68. Catherine Cubbin et al., "Neighborhood Context and Sexual Behaviors among Adolescents: Findings from the National Longitudinal Study of

Adolescent Health," *Perspectives on Sexual and Reproductive Health* 37, no. 3 (September 2005): 125–34; Project on Human Development in Chicago Neighborhoods, "Neighborhood Matters: Selected Findings from the Project on Human Development in Chicago Neighborhoods," December 6, 2005, www.hms.harvard.edu/chase/projects/chicago/ news/annual/MA41_Neighbor_Matters.pdf. (This resource is no longer available at its original URL, but related material may be found at the Inter-university Consortium for Political and Social Research's Project on Human Development in Chicago Neighborhoods at www.icpsr.umich .edu/icpsrweb/PHDCN.)

69. *Medline Plus/Merriam-Webster Medical Dictionary,* s.v. "risk," http:// c.merriam-webster.com/medlineplus/risk.

70. "Sexual Risk Behaviors: HIV, STD, & Teen Pregnancy Prevention," Division of Adolescent and School Health, 2016, www.cdc.gov/ healthyyouth/sexualbehaviors.

71. Kristin Anderson Moore and Jonathan F. Zaff, "Building a Better Teenager: A Summary of 'What Works' in Adolescent Development," *Child Trends Research Brief* 2002–57 (November 2002), https://public .health.oregon.gov/HealthyPeopleFamilies/Youth/AdolescentGrowthDevel opment/Documents/buildingabetterteenager.pdf.

72. Morris Green and Judith S. Palfrey, eds., "Appendix L: Sexually Transmitted Disease Prevention and Screening," in *Bright Futures: Guidelines for Health Supervision of Infants, Children, and Adolescents,* 2nd ed. (Arlington, VA: National Center for Maternal and Child Health, 2000), 319; "Population Reports: Meeting the Needs of Young Adults," *Family Planning Programs,* J, no. 41 (October 1995): 1.

73. See, e.g., the proposed Healthy People 2020 objectives, which include responsible sexual behavior among the leading health indicators for public health goals, www.healthypeople.gov/2010/hp2020/Objectives/ TopicAreas.aspx.

74. American Academy of Pediatrics, Jonathan D. Klein, and the Committee on Adolescence, "Adolescent Pregnancy: Current Trends and Issues," *Pediatrics* 116, no. 1 (July 2005): 281–86.

75. National Campaign to Prevent Teen Pregnancy, "Teens and Oral Sex," 5.

76. Suzanne Ryan, Jennifer Manlove, and Kerry Franzetta, "The First Time: Characteristics of Teens' First Sexual Relationships," *Child Trends Research Brief* 2003–16 (August 2003), www.childtrends.org/wp-content/ uploads/2003/08/First-Time.pdf.

77. Deborah L. Tolman, *Dilemmas of Desire: Teenage Girls Talk about Sexuality* (Cambridge, MA: Harvard University Press, 2002), 188.

78. S. Lilliana Escobar-Chaves et al., "Impact of the Media on Adolescent Sexual Attitudes and Behaviors," *Pediatrics* 116, no. 1 (July 2005): S303–26.

79. Rebecca L. Collins et al., "Watching Sex on Television Predicts Adolescent Initiation of Sexual Behavior," *Pediatrics* 114, no. 3 (September 3, 2004): e280–89.

80. Steven C. Martino et al., "Exposure to Degrading versus Nondegrading Music Lyrics and Sexual Behavior Among Youth," *Pediatrics* 118, no. 2 (August 2006): e430–41.

81. Guzman et al., "Telling It Like It Is," 2.

82. Heather Fish, Jennifer Manlove, and Kristin Anderson Moore, "What Works for Adolescent Sexual and Reproductive Health," 4, 12–35.

83. *College Students' Perceptions of Libraries and Information Resources* (Dublin, OH: Online Computer Library Center, 2006), 5, 2–8.

84. Emily Knox, "Censorship and Religious Reading: An Institutional Approach," presentation, Libraries in the History of Print Culture Conference, Madison, WI, September 10–12, 2010.

85. See, e.g., ideas at "Media," The National Campaign to Prevent Teen and Unplanned Pregnancy, 2016, https://thenationalcampaign.org/featured -topics/media.

86. Kendra S. Albright and Karen W. Gavigan, eds., Sarah Petrulis, illustrator, *AIDS in the End Zone* (Columbia: University of South Carolina Press, 2014).

87. Holly Hibner, "AIDS in the End Zone," Awful Library Books, http:// awfullibrarybooks.net/aids-in-the-end-zone.

88. Mindy E. Scott et al., "Characteristics of Young Adult Sexual Relationships."

89. "Ohio v. Akron Center for Reproductive Health Inc.," American Psychological Association, www.apa.org/about/offices/ogc/amicus/ohio .aspx; Heather Boonstra and Elizabeth Nash, "Minors and the Right to Consent to Health Care," *Guttmacher Report on Public Policy* 3, no. 4 (August 2000), www.guttmacher.org/pubs/tgr/03/4/gr030404.html.

90. John Berry, "If Words Will Never Hurt Me, Then—?" *Library Journal* 117 (January 1992): 6, quoted in Edward Evans, *Developing Library and Information Center Collections,* 4th ed. (Englewood, CO: Libraries Unlimited, 2000), 565.

Four

Changing Minds

The ambiguous, slightly self-mocking status update—"It's complicated"—is ever more apt as a description of what experts tell us about the teen brain. At the same time that scientists and psychologists now reject the developmental scheme outlined by Jean Piaget in 1928, which equated the dawn of adolescence with cognitive maturity, new studies are just reaching explanatory power. This means that librarians must accept that, while older explanations of adolescence have been discarded, new ideas about cognition and maturation are still in their early stages. There are newly important conclusions, though, about how the brain changes and how daily choices can affect teens. One line that resonates in the midst of changing notions about what happens during adolescence and what it means to arrive at legal and social markers of maturity is researcher Jay Giedd's assurance: "The teen brain isn't broken," he said. "It's just different."[1]

A number of fields and professions have already incorporated the results of Giedd's pioneering research into their expectations of adolescents. Alabama attorney Ebony Howard, who won a court case against police for discrimination against African-American teens, has described the importance of how we think about teens and their capacity for learning. Adolescents are still young people, she said, who are learning "how to be citizens, how to be adults." Because of their youth, they won't get it right every time. "During that process, they will make mistakes," she acknowledges, arguing that mistakes made in the process of maturing shouldn't be met the same way adult misconduct is.[2] Her work represents one example of how research on adolescent brain development is shifting the perspectives and the actions of our potential partners who work with teens, and librarians need to engage these paradigms. Some explanation of how we've arrived at this point, the conclusions of cognitive scientists, and specific subjects that concern researchers and policy makers follow.

Howard and cognitive science researchers recognize that some people resist the new characterization of teens as individuals whose brains are still maturing. There are advocates for young people who fear that reassessments of teens' cognitive development will erode teens' rights or are somehow inherently belittling. These concerns are misplaced. Researcher Laurence Steinberg has commented, "Adolescence is not a deficiency, a disease, or a disability, but it is a stage of life when people are less mature than they will be when they are adults." He explains, "Pointing this out is no more biased against teenagers than it is prejudiced against babies to note that infants can't walk as well as preschoolers."[3] Another caveat is that studying the brain does "not reduce adolescence to little more than a network of neurons, to suggest that everything that adolescents do is dictated by biology alone."[4] These studies, rather, ultimately aim to create better conditions for and interactions with teens. A number of the voices involved in explaining what we now know about teens' brains are parents themselves, people who are deeply invested in helping teens achieve their goals.

A bit of context may help explain why absolutes are missing from newer understandings of the brain. Brain studies have gained prominence in recent decades in part because, within the last twenty years, scientists recognized new ways of using technology to analyze the brain. This is a relatively short horizon for research, and it's not unheard of for an idea that was tentatively accepted after initial research to be modified or more staunchly affirmed a few years later. Legendary stories of scientific discovery emphasize the moment an idea emerges and insight crystalizes—the eureka moment when Archimedes leapt from his bathtub with the understanding of how to measure volume and density.[5] The reality is that scientific discoveries result from sometimes lengthy processes and repeated efforts to assess what happens in the world. Also, because the data are so new, we may lack practice-oriented conclusions that resonate in our daily interactions with teens. While work by specialists in psychology, psychiatry, and neuroscience is key to what we know about how the brain develops, many still believe that "even the wide range of recently uncovered changes will not, in the end, prove to be the full story of the dynamic teenage brain."[6]

A colleague who studies learning and the brain once told me, "Many areas of the brain are engaged in even the simplest of tasks." Thus, although places in the brain are still associated with functions like speech and balance, scientists consider the way a core area may be supplemented by or work in conjunction with another part of the brain. Familiarity with regions of the brain remains useful when considering the recent scientific research since those reference points are still used, even as the thinking about their purpose and scope changes. Generally, the anatomy of the brain is described by its larger components. As physician Frances Jensen explains, "Structurally, the human brain is divided into four lobes: frontal (top front), parietal (top back), temporal (sides), and occipital (back)." There are "specialized regions for each of the senses," regions within the lobes that govern our abilities and actions.[7] The *cerebellum* is associated with the control of movement but also with aspects of thinking that involve "precise timing, such as playing a musical instrument."[8] Recent research has indicated the importance of the cerebellum's role in coordinating thinking, whereas older models understood it as primarily involved in controlling physical activity.[9] It also plays a role in the processing of social cues.[10]

In almost every instance, the ways the brain functions are more complicated than had been thought. In response, some researchers prefer to talk about the brain in terms of distributed functioning and neural pathways, involving cellular-level functions that enable the brain to transmit information to its constituent parts. Readers interested in terms and anatomy may consult the Brain Basics section of the collaborative BrainFacts.org site, but the terms below will be helpful to nonspecialists who want to know more about the changes that take place during adolescence.[11]

> **Neurons** are nerve cells involved in conveying information.

> **Dendrites** are branchlike structures that allow the transmission of information among neurons.

> **Synapses** are a particular sort of small space between neurons across which information is carried by chemical impulses. The chemical signals are then converted to electrical ones in order to continue transmission.

> **Myelin,** a fatty substance that covers connecting tissue in the brain, aids the speed of transmission. "An electrical charge travels a hundred times faster on a myelinated axon than an unmyelinated one, reaching speeds of more than 200 miles an hour," according to a science editor for the *New York Times*. Levels of myelin change dramatically during adolescence.[12]

Discussion of the parts of the brain persists because one of the chief findings to emerge from neuroscience was that some areas mature more slowly than others. In particular, the *frontal lobe,* one part of the cerebrum, is regarded as both important to reasoned decision making and slower to acquire adult properties. Its role in impulse control, risk evaluation, and understanding consequences and goals has significance for the myriad independent choices teens make every day. Jensen describes a back-to-front progression in the way "the connectivity of the brain slowly moves from the back of the brain to the front."[13] Another explanation of this facet of cognitive development offers this perspective: "It is not that these tasks cannot be done before young adulthood, but rather that it takes less effort, and hence is more likely to happen" when connections and maturation are more complete.[14] The final stages of the process often described, colloquially, as wiring are believed to happen during a person's early and mid-twenties, the time of life that most behavioral and social scientists refer to as young adulthood.

We often hear the sometimes startling take-away about how long it takes to achieve mature functioning from the research being done on teens' brain development. What is also true but sees less attention is that the changes taking place during adolescence mean the teen brain processes messages swiftly and efficiently. Its responsiveness during this time is distinctive. Laurence has written that "adolescence is the brain's *last* period of especially heightened malleability, . . . a period of brain growth that is far more sensitive to experience than anyone previously imagined."[15] Habits of thought and activity, where the pathways are used more often, are enhanced by that usage. Connections and specialization, then, are two other aspects of brain function that are highly significant in adolescence because the choices a teen makes during these years will enhance these patterns. Thus, the changes taking place in the teen brain may represent an open door, a time when new paths for information processing can more readily be developed.

These ideas, which result from the work of researchers in multiple specialties, challenge us to begin rethinking how we engage young people's minds in libraries and other information-rich environments. Science does not simply tell us what to do. New information relevant to, though not produced by, our field can enrich how we think about the needs of younger users. Any number of LIS studies have observed teens' information-seeking activities, relying on interviews, journals, and often teens' own accounts of their intentions, to clarify researchers' observations. The resulting findings can be augmented by ideas about the underlying cognitive changes that play a part in users' behaviors. Respecting teens' voices and their perspectives on library services remains important but can be interpreted with reference to scientific understandings of the complex changes taking place inside adolescents' heads. These studies offer us context for our policies, programming, and individual interactions with younger users.

Still, we don't want to leap to unwarranted conclusions about what this science means. It has been argued, for example, that the brain changes taking place during adolescence "provide librarians with an opportunity to turn young adults into lifelong readers and library users."[16] In actuality, there is little direct evidence for this claim. It might be more accurate to say that cognitive habits of the teen years typically turn into lasting ones, so that an adolescent uninterested in reading during these formative years is unlikely to acquire a passion for novels or nonfiction later in life. A teen who enjoys reading, on the other hand, is likely to continue reading in adult life.

Recent studies of cognition help us reflect on the environments for young adults that we create in our libraries. We can consider whether simple changes in our interactions with young people could respond to the changing nature of their decision making and communication skills. For example, one researcher has observed that a developmental lull makes repetition essential to ensuring teens will remember important messages; it's not that they're ignoring us or are unfocused, only that other parts of their brains are more engaged than the ones that help them hang onto such messages.[17] Professional conversations about how contemporary information about teens can help us connect with them have barely begun and need more effort.

Few researchers endorse the sort of biological determinism that posits a particular act, message, or structure as a solution to a problem. Many prominent brain experts, though, argue that the implications of newly demonstrated changes taking place during puberty and early adulthood should alter the way we think about adolescence. We are learning that the brain is continually changing and that knowledge, in turn, directs attention to the nature of teens' experiences during this uniquely important phase of development. Youth advocates have asked that we design library spaces that will appeal to adolescents and that we consult teens during the process of planning services for them. Scientists, by offering insights into factors involved in young people's perspectives on and responses to the world around them, can help librarians evaluate what teens tell us. One example is that we have explanations, now, for the differences in behavior that result from decisions made in dynamic, peer-focused contexts and what teens do individually. Research has the power to challenge and refine our ideas about teens' use of libraries' services and resources.

The Field of Neuroscience

Many of the researchers who offer us new ideas about teens' brains are neuroscientists. According to the Society for Neuroscience, neuroscience is a relatively new yet burgeoning specialty linking biology, medicine, and other disciplines. On one level, neuroscience is the scientific study of the brain. More precisely, the society says, "Neuroscience, the study of the nervous system, advances the understanding of human thought, emotion, and behavior." The society identifies three key areas of research undertaken by neuroscientists: "Through their research, neuroscientists work to describe the human brain and how it functions normally, determine how the nervous system develops, matures and maintains itself through life, and find ways to prevent or cure many devastating neurological and psychiatric disorders." It is a complex type of research, in part because a human body contains approximately a hundred billion neurons. From its modern origins circa 1969, the field has expanded significantly in the twenty-first century.[18] ∎

CHANGE AND THE TEEN BRAIN

What is the single most important finding to emerge from all this research? Chiefly, it is the repudiation of the assumption, which had prevailed for many years, that the teen brain is essentially an adult brain. Researchers agree that while most previous developmental models assumed that the brain changed little once young people arrived at adolescence, a plethora of studies have debunked this once-bedrock notion. One researcher's clever quip encapsulates the matter nicely: "Most people thought [the teen brain] was pretty much like an adult's, only with fewer miles on it. The problem with this assumption is that it was wrong."[19]

The old view held that major change was a feature of the child's mind, and teens differed from the very young by their intellectual similarity to adults. It's easy to surmise how research informed by observation of behavior could create this perception. Readily apparent developmental milestones that reflected cognitive change— say, language acquisition, represented first by the utterance of sounds, then the approximation of words, the joining of words into phrases, the construction of sentences, and so on—happened in childhood. The cognitive changes in young adults—such as the development of a larger and more sophisticated vocabulary or the realization that nuances of meaning aid creative expression—seemed less significant in comparison to those of the early years. Even recent researchers have remarked, "The cognitive changes in adolescence are not as significant and dramatic as the ones present in early childhood . . . and adolescence marks a refinement, rather than an emergence, of these abilities."[20] Research conditions reinforced the idea that because teens looked and seemed more or less capable of acting like adults, their brain development was nearly completed, and so the developmental stages proposed by Piaget ended in early adolescence with the acquisition of abstract reasoning skills, or the ability to reason about ideas as well actualities. Many scientific theories mirrored this thinking about the adolescent brain as a more or less fixed, rather than fluctuating, subject.

These days, research relying on new tools and techniques of study indicates that the changes taking place in adolescent brains are dynamic rather than subtle. Studies have clearly demonstrated periods of significant growth in adolescent brains, notably shortly before the onset of puberty. These changes have been compared to the physical growth spurt seen in adolescents' bodies, but researchers have found that the processes manifesting themselves in adolescence begin years beforehand.[21] This research demonstrates that several stereotypically teen characteristics—among them impulsive or risky behavior, explosive responses to even mild comments, a night owl's reluctance to rise early in the morning, and episodes of forgetfulness—are linked to changes in structure and chemical levels in the brain. Further, it is thought that this results in changes in motivation. The teen brain is in transition as the proliferation and then pruning of neural pathways provides teens with new approaches to problem solving. It is not enough, though, for those pathways to be available; teens must learn to use them, and to use them routinely, to achieve adult patterns of thought and action. This is often a process of trial and error. In short, irksome teen behavior may be linked to ongoing brain development.

Yet researchers are cautious about simply blaming troublesome teen behaviors on ongoing brain development. It has been pointed out that some adults, whose brains have completed these late-occurring phases of development, can still be prone to rash and at times unpleasant conduct.[22] The ways biology interacts with environment, specifically the way environmental conditions may either facilitate or discourage biological inclinations, have also been noted in the reasoning about behavior and maturation. For example, the contemporary environment, through its electric-powered, multi-media entertainment and information options, allows teens to engage their natural drives for stimulation and late-night activity with relative ease.

The brain development that takes place during adolescence increases young people's abilities to understand the world around them and to respond reflectively, yet this development also has limitations. Thinking of development as an incremental process affected by environment and other conditions, rather than as an on-off switch that suddenly and dramatically changes teens' perceptions or skills, is key to understanding teens' attitudes and actions. Brain development, then, is only one factor contributing to young people's behavior during a time of life that is popularly characterized as turbulent or unpredictable.

When I've talked about some of these findings with my students, they are quick to observe that younger children have some of the skills and intellectual abilities now thought to be points of weakness for teenagers. I once described research that found disparities between adolescents' and adults' abilities to interpret facial expressions. To many of the students in that class, this didn't make sense because they knew that young children could associate facial expressions and feelings. If a child can perform certain cognitive tasks, why would someone approaching adulthood find the same tasks difficult? The answers to this question are complex. Researchers have identified periods of recurring changes in the brain, or times when a type of processing gains rapidly just before adolescence, enters a period of stasis during the main teen years, then resumes a high-level of function during a person's early 20s.[23]

It is common, perhaps even desirable, to think of young people's development as a trajectory of increasingly sophisticated abilities. The way we talk about early childhood—a baby's progression from crawling to walking, from social smiles to babbling before uttering first words—reflects this sort of assumption. Yet young children sometimes continue to depend on earlier habits of locomotion and speech rather than make immediate and exclusive use of their newly developed skills. Adolescents, too, often waver between moments of maturity and behavior that belies their nearness to adulthood. In other words, just because you see a teen demonstrate good judgment in one situation doesn't mean that she will do so every time.

Maturation involves multiple processes that do not begin—or end—at the same time. As with physical development, cognitive changes that characterize adolescence begin earlier in girls than in boys. Also, some aspects of brain development recur; they are not completed in a single execution. And as scientists have cautioned, new cognitive skills are only one component of teens' actions; changes in the brain make an increasing array of activities possible but do not cause a particular outcome. Researchers now cite the importance of context, the moment or the environment in which a teen functions, as a critical aspect of how his decisions unfold.

Researchers will continue working to understand the implications of their discoveries to date as well as endeavoring to respond to new questions. Some things are clear—specific parts of the brain are still in development even as teens reach the end of the period that librarians have labeled young adulthood. Some things are not, like all the specific entailments of that ongoing change. As the producer of a documentary examining the work of National Institutes of Health neuroscientist Jay Giedd and other researchers observed, these findings enrich our understanding of adolescence as a time when cognitive development is taking place, making it "a time of both heightened opportunity and risk."[24] After scientists marvel at the implications of the new knowledge they are gaining, they note that the ability to draw conclusions about the implications of these changes is still unfolding. Some of the earliest data that pointed to the malleability of the teen brain came from Giedd's analysis of data revealed by MRIs in 1997. The first report on this data, the work of Giedd and his coinvestigators, was published in 1999. That data showed significant growth at a time when such growth was assumed to be essentially over, instigating a powerful reexamination of assumptions about brain development. In the scientific world, the time since Giedd's first report is a rather brief period to be in possession of revolutionary knowledge, both to know that things are different from what we had supposed and to understand the full meaning of that knowledge, which is still being generated.

Questions necessarily arise when fundamental ideas are revised. What are librarians to do with young adult users, whose brains are more complex and malleable—and more vulnerable—than we had previously thought? How do these new pronouncements about teens' maturity, or the newly uncovered limits thereof, affect our advocacy for their rights to private, uncensored, and independent library use? Librarians who advocate for teens have argued that younger users should be offered full access to all materials, included in discussions about meeting their needs, and respected as adults. The assumption has been that young people's maturity meant that they were capable of making sound judgments about their information and recreational reading needs, even, or especially, with regard to potentially controversial and sensitive matters. Do the findings of Giedd and other researchers indicate that our faith in teens' abilities is too generous? What sorts of services and resources are appropriate for a young person when the physical structure of that individual's brain is still under construction? In other words, are our post-1967 professional ideals and policies congruent with post-1997 research on adolescents' cognitive abilities?

The research taking place offers new information about invisible processes occurring in the minds of teens and tweens who visit our libraries. Giedd has said, for instance, that given what we know about the adolescent brain, it seems inappropriate to ask teens to make adult decisions, and attorneys and activists like Bryan Stevenson have used this research to advocate that teens embroiled in the legal system not be subject to the same conditions and punishments as adults.[25] At minimum, this expert testimony gives us reasons to revisit our services and policies pertaining to this group of library users. Motivated by user feedback and environmental scans, libraries have begun to change their policies and planning for teens, looking for alternatives to fines and creating spaces where teen activity, should it become rambunctious or even just noisy, won't be disruptive to other library users. These professional paths seem congruent with what we are learning about how teens think and respond to the world around them.

INSIGHTS AND EXPLANATIONS
What's Going On in a Teen's Brain

We've all had moments of witnessing teens choose some seemingly inexplicable course of action, of wondering what was going on in their heads. Now scientists are able to offer some insight into exactly that because specialized MRIs allow researchers to see adolescents' brains at work. Efforts to understand what parts of the brain do while adolescent changes play out have advanced knowledge about what growth takes place during the teens and which behaviors may be affected. This focus on structures and behaviors ignores disciplinary lines in an effort to focus on hypotheses and conclusions of interest to librarians. Doing so follows the lead of researchers in this area who seek interdisciplinary connections to enhance their knowledge by learning from each other.[26]

It is important to emphasize that few researchers believe the brain alone determines teen behavior. Cognitive capabilities, although admittedly significant, are just one factor that shapes young people's actions and interacts with environmental factors like education and culture. Further, emotional states and relationships with caregivers also factor into teen behavior, particularly in when it comes to risk taking. Stages of brain development affect or even limit teens' abilities to reason and to form judgments, but they do not predestine particular choices.

Giedd's research is often cited as groundbreaking in clarifying how we understand teens' developmental changes. His work involves taking MRI scans of adolescents' brains at regular intervals in order to assess changes taking place as young people grow and mature. This research project began in 1991, and by 1997 some of the first indications of the profoundly different truth about the nature of brain development were becoming apparent. The findings, created in conjunction and consultation with other researchers who relied on the same data, are the basis for revising our understanding of how teens' brains work and mature.

Giedd demonstrated that adolescents' brains undergo recurrent development, chiefly through alternating cycles of proliferation and then pruning of connections within the brain. Changes were observed largely in the prefrontal cortex, the part of the brain associated with reasoning, with a round of rapid growth beginning shortly before puberty. This has been interpreted as an indication that the executive control center of the brain, the region that governs decision making, is still being formed. Key tasks that rely on the frontal cortex include planning, foreseeing consequences, organizing, and problem solving.[27] To see the part of the brain that is central to all these activities as in the midst of change, rather than fully operational, offers new perspective on stereotypical teen behaviors.

Another fact determined by Giedd and the other researchers who examined a succession of brain scans of young people was that the brain takes a long time to mature. Researchers now believe that the brain acquires adult form when an individual is approximately twenty-five years old. Another researcher, also a parent, has commented, "With teenagers, it's especially hard to remember that their brains are developing because they look like adults. . . . But even though teenagers have the bodies of adults, they are not adults."[28] Teens, especially younger ones, are still developing brain mechanisms that will allow them to check impulsive responses and to think rationally in the midst of exciting or compelling situations. Giedd has said, "This whole concept of adolescence being stretched out longer, not just socially, but biologically was an important impact from the imaging studies."[29] Another expert argues we should redefine *adolescence* based on these findings, seeing it as a stage that takes place between the ages of ten and twenty-five.[30]

Similarly, experiences with older teens have led some librarians to question whether YA services might continue after adolescents reach the age of eighteen. Young adult librarians who have gotten to know their teen patrons sometimes offer stories about first-year college students who return to the young adult desk when home on vacation, seeking out the library staff members who were so helpful only months ago. To these librarians, teens who recently graduated from high school may not seem much different from those who haven't yet gone through this rite of passage. Recent scientific research on the brain contributes to the notion that high school graduation, while it may be a defining moment in a teen's life, doesn't turn our eighteen-year-old users into adult patrons, and it supports arguments that young adult services should be intended for any young person who arrives at our service desks rather than limited to those who fall within the historically designated age range. Cognitive research might encourage librarians to explore which services truly must be age restricted and which can be usefully adapted to changing contemporary situations.

The increasing-then-decreasing number of connections in the brain has many implications. Neuroscientists use the term *plasticity* to refer to the brain's ability to change or to develop new patterns of conveying information. Plasticity has been implicated in some areas of learning, such as language acquisition, but is less clearly understood in others, such as the ability to control emotions. Yet, researchers believe that the brain's capacity to change creates both opportunities and vulnerabilities during the adolescent years.[31] This makes adolescence an extremely important time of life.[32] The heightened plasticity of teens' brains means their behaviors and aptitudes are particularly malleable; however, that malleability is not indefinite. The phrase "use it or lose it" has been taken as a sort of shorthand for what happens during the brain's development in adolescence. Giedd sees adolescence as a time when the brain is working out ways to function effectively and efficiently.[33] When some activities become a routine part of a young person's life, those pathways in the brain are reinforced. The less-used pathways decline and eventually disappear. Giedd explained it this way: "If a teen is doing music or sports or academics, those are the cells and connections that will be hard-wired. If they're lying on the couch or playing video games or MTV, those are the cells and connections that are going [to] survive."[34] Scientists call this pattern of brain development pruning because the earlier, preadolescent proliferation of connections is reduced, and they acknowledge that there is more to learn about this aspect of adolescent brain development.

Pruning may be viewed as a process of refining important capabilities, like "inhibition control and working memory, or the ability to hold information in your head when there is competing information."[35] It involves complex tasks: teens must not simply suppress their desires to act on impulse, but also learn to feel positively about activities such as working toward goals, enhancing strategic decision making, and complying with social norms.[36] Researchers observe that, for teens, making the best choice can be difficult because their sense of reward in the here and now outweighs a far more abstract, remote one. Jensen explains, "In general, teen brains get more of a sense of reward than adult brains, and . . . the release of and response to dopamine is enhanced in the teen brain."[37]

Plasticity, then, is also of interest because it appears to have consequences for risk-taking behavior. Risk taking is a challenging aspect of adolescent behavior because it is strongly rooted in the conditions of that time of life. Ronald E. Dahl, a researcher with the University of Pittsburgh, stated,

> Adolescence often contains the developmental roots of lifetime problems with nicotine dependence, alcohol and drug use, poor health habits, relationship difficulties, and failure to develop skills or knowledge leading to a productive job or career. Trajectories are set in adolescence that can have a major impact in life, and there are reasons to believe that altering these trajectories in positive ways prior to adulthood can have a larger scale effect than the same intervention applied later in the lifespan.

Dahl is among the researchers who have demonstrated that teens' inclinations toward risk taking vary considerably. Without distraction, an audience, or strong emotions, they perform ideally, but under other conditions it is significantly harder for them to make the choices that are in their own best interests. His words are clear:

> Adolescents often appear to be relatively good at making decisions under conditions of low arousal and cool emotions. This same highly intelligent youth, under intense emotional arousal, can have a much more difficult time making a responsible choice.[38]

Teens' behavior will vary. The apparent unpredictability of their behavior results from different situations and varying abilities to maintain control as brains and emotions change. While it is sometimes tempting to see teens' inclinations toward risk taking as a result of contemporary culture, researchers indicate that teens have almost always taken chances with activities and ideas that could harm them and disquiet their parents. It has to do with what is taking place biologically, not just the possibilities for entertainment and recreation in contemporary society. The tendency to take risks suggests that adolescence is a critical time because of the long-term implications of what teens do—or don't do—during this part of their lives.

Certainly, it could be argued that new brain research supports youth advocates' contentions that teens should have spaces of their own and access to librarians who are aware of their distinctive needs. Increasing staff members' familiarity with new information about adolescence as a developmental stage is one relatively simple change that can enhance the library environment for teens. Researchers stress that teens need positive, understanding communication. Jensen tells us to "encourage them to try different activities and new ways of thinking about things. . . . Your job isn't to stifle them but rather to help them channel their energies in positive directions."[39] Although aimed at parents, her advice seems suited to libraries, with their arrays of collections and programs. She urges adults to remember that "behavior has to be taken in context" before reacting to seeming provocations or misbehavior.[40]

Because young adult librarians are not the only staff in contact with young people, it may be worthwhile to ask that all public service staff and library policy makers become familiar with reassessments of the adolescent mind. Popular readings, videos, and experts committed to outreach are available to explain these concepts. Information of this sort may help staff manage interactions with teens more productively, equipping them to recognize bursts of noisiness, for example, as lapses of judgment rather than disregard for library rules. Research indicating that teens' brains are undergoing dramatic changes does not necessarily excuse inappropriate activity; it can, however, help frame productive rather than simply confrontational responses. It can also be used to structure library and information environments in ways that meet younger users' needs and minimize potential conflict. If we know that teens are working in groups, for example, and that their interactions will likely grow louder than other library users will readily tolerate, how do we respond? Respecting young adults as we would any other patron would involve making group spaces available to them, much as we offer meeting rooms to our adult patrons. Creating policies that allow equitable access to the full range of library resources serves multiple objectives, including respecting adolescents' rights as library users and accommodating their changing and changeable activities. Another strategy some libraries employ is constructing spaces for young adults with doors that can be closed during noisier, social activities. Employing creative ways to make space for teens' interactions, such as after-hours programming or repurposing little-used areas of the library, minimizes the potential that the sounds of games or excited conversation might carry and disturb patrons whose use of the library is of a more contemplative nature.

Scientific research on the brain has shown that adolescents do not process information—including events and activities in the world around them—the same way adults do. Increasingly, researchers want to understand how teens use their brains differently than adults use theirs. There is a variety of evidence about this, and tests of differences between adolescent and adult responses to stimuli, like potentially dangerous or threatening cues, have been used to learn more about these differences.

If you're a devotee of National Public Radio, you might have heard a broadcast in which a writer told a story about her rebellious teen years: she wanted to go to a late-night showing of the *Rocky Horror Picture Show,* and her mother thought it was far too late for a young teen to be out on her own. The writer described how she blithely invited her mother to go along to the movie, who surprised everyone by agreeing, but then left her mother sitting alone while she sat elsewhere with her friends. She periodically looked back at her prim mother amid the cacophony and outlandish performances that accompanied the movie, and by the expression on her face, she knew that her mother was angry. Years later, the time Mom went to *Rocky Horror Picture Show* was firmly entrenched in the family lore, and enough time had passed that the writer felt inclined to discuss this moment that pitted teen desires against parental control. She learned that where she had thought her mother was angry, her mother was actually frightened by a chaotic and turbulent environment in which she was clearly out of place.

The ending to this story wouldn't surprise Deborah Yurgelun-Todd, a Harvard researcher who has compared teen and adult abilities to interpret facial expressions. She found that, while adults correctly read a person's nonverbal cues in order to differentiate between fear, anger, and other emotional states, adolescents routinely got it wrong. Younger people often misunderstood the facial expressions that reflected attitude and emotion in this experiment. The younger the teen, the more likely it was that interpretive difficulties would prevail: "Kids under the age of 14 often characterized the facial expressions as sad, angry, or confused rather than fearful. Older teenagers answered correctly more often." Yurgelun-Todd was able to identify the cause for the resulting miscommunication: whereas adults' prefrontal cortexes were active during the experiment, teens' prefrontal cortexes were far less involved. Although involvement of the prefrontal cortex increased as the teens grew older, they literally relied on another part of their brains to evaluate what they were seeing. The conclusion was that teens' inability to rely on the developing prefrontal cortex hindered their ability to make sense of others' nonverbal messages.[41]

The emerging research is something librarians should attend to, especially in light of studies in the field that show some portion of young people have negative perceptions of library staff members and find them unwelcoming. The OCLC surveyed U.S. teens ages fourteen to seventeen and reported on respondents' impressions of libraries. The numerous complaints about librarians' attitudes toward young people ranged from the evocative, if ungrammatical, "Be more friendlier" to a somewhat more articulate plea: "Have the librarians seem more approachable, less stiff and imposing."[42] Even among their slightly older peers given the same survey, concerns about whether library staff were approachable resonated. Of the 9 percent of college-aged respondents who commented on staffing, many were also intimidated or disconcerted by librarians. College students described librarians much as their younger peers did: they asked for "nicer" and "friendlier" staff.[43] The fact that younger users might misinterpret facial expressions that signal perhaps ambiguous states, like concentration or surprise, is a clear take-away lesson from the complex and often conditional findings on adolescent brains. One practice that librarians could adopt to ease negative perceptions and make younger users feel welcome: focus on patrons in public service areas and smile to greet them.

Other researchers have argued the importance of sleep to teens' abilities to make sound decisions and function well generally. More than one researcher has concluded that "sleep deprivation can affect mood, performance, attention, learning, behavior, and biological functions."[44] Mary Carskadon has provided data indicating that teens' tendencies to become night owls is attributable to their biology rather than recalcitrance. She has also found that teens, not unlike younger children, require more sleep than adults. Her calculation is that adolescents, on average, need 9.25 hours a night. Continued research on adolescents' sleep patterns confirms that most U.S. teens do not get enough sleep.[45] Melatonin, a chemical needed for sleep, is secreted in teens' bodies later in the evening than it is in adults or pre-adolescents and, in turn remains in their bodies later in the morning.[46] Other aspects of sleep are notable in addition to the adjusted body clocks that seem to be a normal feature of adolescence. Experiments conducted by a number of researchers have demonstrated multiple poor outcomes that result from sleep deprivation. Among them is that teens' abilities to perform well and react appropriately to stimuli are impaired.[47] Teens' night-owl tendency is something librarians might be asked to consider.

At one library conference I attended, a city administrator compared Starbucks and libraries. He observed that coffee shops and other late-night spaces where teens could interact were thriving, while libraries were closed during late hours when teens were looking for places to go. Later hours, he suggested, would attract teens to libraries, and wouldn't the library be a better place for them? Aside from the challenges of financing additional hours of service, this kind of suggestion should be evaluated in light of research on teens' sleep. Given teens' biological sleep patterns, offering library services later into the night seems reasonable. Yet, extending service hours also would have the potential of appearing to support some teens' tendency to get less sleep than they need. Balancing what teens seem to want with what might be in their best interests can be challenging and requires serious assessment.

Promoting the library's online resources to younger users is one means of bridging the gap between teens' tendency toward late-night activity and many public libraries' limited hours. While such an approach dodges the issue of the library as a place for teens, it gives teens unaware of this option access to full-text articles, e-books, and audio downloads—at least some of the resources the library has to offer. Despite teens' reputation as net-savvy individuals, recent surveys reveal that many younger users are not aware of library web pages and e-resources. Librarians shouldn't assume that younger patrons will find the library's database page or the well-crafted online guide to completing a science fair project that staff spent hours creating. For teens to take advantage of libraries' online resources, it will be necessary to promote such materials off-line, including through partnerships with teachers and teacher-librarians.

Discussions about teen maturity invariably resort to the idea that hormones cause teens' unpredictable or undesirable conduct. It's a sort of widely repeated popular wisdom; however, this take on teen motivation isn't true. Although such theories were popular until the end of the twentieth century, most researchers now discredit them. Simple measures of hormone levels disprove the contention. One researcher observes that "teenagers don't have higher hormone levels than young adults—they just react differently to hormones." Those hormones, most experts believe, represent only one difference.[48] It has been reported that "there appears to be little *direct* relationship between hormone levels and measures of behavior or emotion," and "we now understand that high levels of sex hormones are not the cause of emotional problems in adolescents."[49] Instead, researchers have located one source—but only one—of unpredictable or undesirable conduct.

This source is a teen's environment. The research acknowledges that the conditions in which a teen lives and learns are developmentally important. This research both offers information and poses challenges for librarians who work with adolescents. It explains causes for teens' changing behavior while downplaying or dismissing other factors once thought to be involved in teens' development. It suggests issues for librarians to consider as they reevaluate policies that affect younger users without dictating the course of the resulting decisions. In this context, it seems important for librarians to direct their attention to the nature of the environment they create for adolescent patrons.

A Conversation with Ronald Dahl[50]

Talking about new understandings of the adolescent mind encompasses ideas as diverse as developmental psychologist Jean Piaget and graduated driver's licenses. Yet Ronald Dahl makes these and other connections with ease, explaining how what we know about adolescence has changed over the years and what sorts of guidance assist in producing good outcomes for teens today. When Dahl talks about teens, he regularly refers to the "igniting passions" that young people experience during adolescence as well as the roles adults can play in supporting healthy decisions or tempering impetuous ones that might lead to poor consequences.

Dahl's descriptions of adolescence indicate this developmental phase is an important one, in part because of how teens think about themselves. "It's a time when kids are developing a sense of self," he said. "They can imagine themselves in the future. They have feelings about this." These features of teens' emotional lives, which Dahl refers to as "perceived self-narratives," are important.

Adults should pay attention to the way teens talk about themselves, whether young people envision themselves in positive or negative ways. This self-talk has a certain amount of predictive power, Dahl said. "It's a time when the trajectory can shift rapidly. A particular experience in adolescence can really tip that," he said, noting that "a lot of circumstantial evidence" based on individuals' recollections links happenings in the teen years with life choices. Dahl referred to the way adolescents identify a book, a teacher, or an experience as influential: "It's a key time for kids to develop self-narratives."

Why is adolescence distinctive from earlier developmental phases? Dahl attributes change to what psychologists call affect, more familiarly thought of as feelings. "I think that one of the real shifts is an increase in affective systems—emotion, motivation," Dahl said. There is an increased appetite for risk taking and sensation seeking. "The affective shift at puberty creates opportunities as well

Ronald Dahl is the Staunton Professor of Psychiatry and Pediatrics and professor of psychology at the Western Psychiatric Institute and Clinic, University of Pittsburgh.

as vulnerabilities. This can be a passion for really healthy things. At the same time, it's a time of incredible vulnerability," he observed. The capacity for attraction to negative or positive efforts to engage these emotional systems is significant.

"What we're beginning to get some evidence for is this may be like kids learning language," he explained. Dahl offered examples of young people's ability to acquire language more naturally and with greater ease before puberty. He describes this as a "flexibility for language" and said researchers are now asking, "Are there similar aspects of social fluidity, emotional fluidity that are like that?" The aim of answering this kind of question is to be able to alter young people's behaviors in positive ways "before that window is closed," Dahl said.

Researchers are concluding that learning happens more readily at certain stages in one's life cycle. Dahl described a colleague's research, which examined native Japanese speakers' difficulties with discerning sounds made by the letters *r* and *1*. Her work revealed that infants can distinguish between those sounds and that the ability erodes later in life. Although it is difficult, adults can be coached to learn the difference between *r* and *1* sounds. It's time consuming, he said, and involves a great deal of effort. Further, in adults, a different part of the brain is involved in learning to distinguish one sound from the other. "The route to making the change is less natural. It takes more work," Dahl commented. "You get a lot more bang for the buck when you can intervene early, when there's more plasticity. Adolescence creates unique opportunities."

The studies that produce this kind of awareness of the nature of learning and change are "very multidisciplinary," Dahl observed. "The greatest challenge is integrating across multiple levels." Research on the brain involves studies of every type of being, from rodents to humans, teens to adults. Determining when conclusions can be drawn is other than straightforward and requires the accumulation and rigorous evaluation of a great deal of information. Sleep research demonstrates this complexity.

School principals and policy makers often call him, asking questions like "What time should we start the school day?" and "When should teens be allowed to drive?" The answers are not simple. "You can't blame it on the brain," Dahl said. "There are a whole lot of steps in biological change." Dahl said that in adolescence, two biological drives shift at the same time: teens are naturally inclined to stay up later, yet they also need more sleep. This results in the readily observable teen habits of adopting late bedtimes and sleeping in. In the United States, Dahl said, the average bedtime for an older teen is 11:30 P.M. on a school night. The interaction of the two biological drives, in tandem with the contemporary environment that facilitates late-night activities—as opposed to an earlier era, for example, when any late-night work or play would have been done by flickering candlelight—means there is no single factor or right answer that explains the late-bedtime–sleeping-in dynamic, Dahl explained. "There's this whole set of things."

"The research sheds new light on mechanistic changes," Dahl said of what he and others are learning about the adolescent brain. Because changes are multiple, labeling one element as a causal factor is often inappropriate. "One needs to have rigor at different levels for different types of research," Dahl commented. Piaget, whose developmental stages have often framed LIS concepts of youth, is now regarded as a historical figure, he said. The investigations undertaken by Piaget consisted of observing his own children and reflecting on what he saw. These efforts, though empirical, don't hold up to the scrutiny of scientific research. "Things have changed," Dahl said.

Essentially, according to Dahl, what policy makers want to know is "At what age are kids old enough to be given freedom?" In recent years, this has been asked about driving. The answer involves balance, rather than prohibitions, he said. Some people have assumed that if the brain isn't fully developed in sixteen-year-olds, Dahl summarized, then making teens wait two more years will enable them to gain more maturity. One problem he identifies in this assumption is that the amount of change taking place in those two years is not enough to make a difference. Dahl observed that adolescent drivers don't tend to have many accidents in the first six months behind the wheel; the number of accidents spikes afterward. This occurs because during these first six months teens have permits and drive with a parent or other adult who helps monitor and guide the judgment calls that are a routine part of driving. When the teen starts to drive alone, accidents increase. The young person's behavior or thinking hasn't changed, he said, but the external controls have.

These facts have led some people to ask why teens should be allowed to drive when they are experiencing, biologically, increased tendencies toward risk taking and sensation seeking. There are important reasons for encouraging and supporting teens' learning of all sorts at this time, among them the ease with which young people can acquire new knowledge and skills. Further, understanding when to hesitate or defer an action is part of the critical learning that teens engage in during adolescence. Dahl said that at the same time that inclinations associated with risk decrease, so do more natural periods for learning because plasticity is reduced simultaneously. Graduated licenses are a solution that both allows teens to gain driving skills and provides support for their decision-making processes. "They need to have some freedom or they'll never develop regulatory controls," he said.

The overarching principle, in Dahl's opinion, is that teens must learn to control their own emotions and mental processes. Adults, though, must support and monitor that learning process. The basic problem people are wrestling with is determining how to offer teens enough freedom to learn while ensuring that they are unlikely to harm themselves or others. Continuing to furnish some degree of monitoring is key to achieving the necessary balance. "You want to give them steps of freedom," Dahl said. "This is a key time for learning how to be independent and to manage their emotions. It's risky to give kids too much freedom too fast." ■

The implications of what scientists have learned about adolescent brain development are many, if indirect. Scientific research, while clarifying our understanding of internal processes taking place during puberty and adolescence, offers guidance rather than simple answers. It suggests we consider more fully the nature of younger users' transition from the children's room to the young adult room and beyond in order to support them as they begin to use more complex and information-rich tools. Providing both high-quality and appealing information resources for young adults must remain a priority, given these developmental conditions.

It indicates we might think strategically about the nature of volunteer training when we have teens and tweens who help in our libraries. Determining what types of training and oversight are appropriate, given the combination of how learning works for teens and what we involve them in doing, can facilitate more successful relationships and better outcomes. Support for and review of volunteers' work, essential in any context, clearly must figure in tasks given to teens. Cindy Welch outlines the rationale and process for creating a meaningful plan for incorporating teen volunteers in meeting libraries' needs, focusing on avenues for success in light of changing knowledge about teens' cognitive development.[51] How we communicate both our objectives and our feedback matters, as research indicates that teens may still be developing their capacity for interpreting interpersonal messages. Some experts advise relying on nonconfrontational messages that direct attention to the problem rather than the person; for instance, instead of telling a teen he has made an error in the course of a project, discussing the system and the cues that seem to have been missed or mistaken are thought to yield better results.

Further, research findings may influence how we think about filtering Internet content or blocking certain online activities. Filtering and blocking may guard young people from sensitive content or unscrupulous individuals in the short term, but these constraints do not aid young people who are still developing their ability evaluate online content. Guidance for young people about assessing the information they find via the Internet and the potential consequences of self-disclosure in online venues is important in light of what is being learned about the brain. Outreach to parents, to help them build their own abilities to work with their children's use of information and communication technologies, would be another option.

As knowledge about the brain accumulates, a further consideration is the ethics of how that information is used. In addition to the scientific research taking place within universities and government institutes, corporate marketing research examines the brain's work in generating, for example, people's attraction to one brand rather than another.[52] Marketing-oriented brain research finds that emotion, rather than rationality, appears to motivate decision making.[53] Some have raised questions about whether marketing based on this type of cognitive picture is unduly intrusive and manipulative.[54] Librarians looking for ways to use brain research to increase the lure of the book and the library should be aware of these types of objections.

CONCLUSION

At the same time that this chapter condenses a rather large amount of research into a relatively few pages, there are several omissions. For instance, the research covered focuses on efforts to understand the development and functioning of normal, healthy teens. Some scientists have put forth the idea that a more thorough understanding of the average teen is needed before work to understand troubled teens can be undertaken effectively. Similarly, issues of brain function in young people with cognitive or other disabilities have not been examined here. Because scientists recognize that many of their findings will be used in establishing new baselines and norms, to date they have focused on healthy teens whose lives are free of obvious complications like disabilities.

Further, this chapter has not given much attention to sex-linked differences in brain development. Giedd and others have indicated that, as with other biological changes, girls experience the onset of adolescence-linked brain development earlier than boys do.[55] Many other matters related to the interactions between biological sex and the brain remain unresolved. One Harvard researcher is accumulating evidence about the possibility that, if there are sex-related differences between boys' and girls' brains, those dissimilarities are not present in infancy or toddlerhood.[56] Her research could suggest that differences are acculturated rather than inherent or that they are associated with later biological processes. Beyond the facts—demonstrated through MRI images—that girls' brains begin to show signs of change before boys' brains do and that there are some other relatively small structural differences, the scientific community is not yet in agreement on the subject of sex-related differences between boys' and girls' brains. The available evidence seems to tilt toward attributing differences to the ways in which families and societies treat children, or at least to interactions between nurture and nature, rather than to purely biological factors. Given librarians' concerns about boys and reading, these ideas are provocative.

Even without delving fully into those areas, the research on adolescent brains offers youth services librarians much to evaluate. Research in LIS and practitioner philosophy has long been guided— implicitly if not explicitly—by assumptions grounded in older developmental models. Emerging theories of adolescent development agree that the teen years, and even some years afterward, are distinctive ones. At the same time that these understandings coincide with library practitioners' aims of recognizing the needs of young adults as unlike those of child or adult patrons, they differ in their recognition of limitations on teens' abilities. Research shows us that adolescents, rather than being the sophisticated and worldly individuals they sometimes appear to be, are still learning how to shape their futures and participate in their communities.

One implication of the research is that "teenagers are not the same as adults in a variety of key areas such as the ability to make sound judgments when confronted by complex situations, the capacity to control impulses, and the ability to plan effectively." This assessment does not denigrate teens, whom researchers describe as "full of promise, often energetic and caring, capable of making many contributions to their communities, and able to make remarkable spurts in intellectual development and learning."[57] The researchers' point is that teens are not yet fully equipped with the brain wiring that will support their ability to make sound choices in contemporary environments that are, by their nature, challenging. A term that has been used to describe what teens need in these circumstances is *scaffolding,* or support structures that allow a guided and supportive transition through developmental processes.[58] As our profession becomes more involved in supporting instruction and skills development, ascertaining how youth services librarians can meet teens where they are and improve their futures is a worthy goal. One researcher has noted that "the problems affecting adolescents in our society are both enormous and complex." He and other scientists seek not only to understand "specific neurobiological changes during adolescent development, but also to broaden our knowledge of how behavioral, familial, and social influences interact."[59] In other words, they do not want to dictate new rules for the care and feeding of teens. They do, however, want to understand how all who are involved with teenagers can work together to ensure positive outcomes for young people. Neuroscientists' discoveries about how teen brains work can guide the ways other professionals work with teens to cultivate their decision-making skills. As a white paper that Giedd coauthored stated, "At a minimum, the data suggest that teens need to be surrounded by adults and institutions that help them learn specific skills and appropriate adult behavior." Yet, this report notes that the "specific systems and practices" that will help teens develop successfully have not yet been identified.[60] Libraries are institutions with the potential to support young people's learning and development, and our professional values place us among the adults and institutions that contribute to adolescents' growth.

Scientists' findings indicate, then, that despite popular perceptions of teens as independent individuals, young people still benefit from adults' involvement in their lives. Interactions with caring and reflective adults are essential to teens, who still need certain kinds of protection and guidance. This challenges us professionally because young people visit libraries for material that not only supports their decision making in everyday life, but also meets their recreational and academic needs. Research suggests that librarians should not assume that tweens and teens are always capable of knowing and acting in their own best interests, although they may do so in some situations. Those working with young people in libraries will need to consider appropriate ways to offer structured choices and assist teens in identifying strategies for making decisions.

In light of the new concept of adolescence, perhaps the greatest challenge to librarians involves reconciling our ideals with the idea that young people are, as some researchers have said, "works in progress."

Young adult librarians and advocates have vigilantly asserted the rights of young adults to be recognized as adults in all but name. The scholarly and practitioner literatures of our field include work that accepts and adapts the research that redefines adolescence, as well as some that, at times angrily, attempts to refute it. The latter attitude, however, seems mired in an indefensible historical perspective that distances us from knowledge accepted by our community partners. In thinking about what new models of adolescent development mean for us and for our patrons, there are several things to remember.

First and foremost, we need to recognize that in the academic disciplines specializing in the study of the brain, Piaget, Freud, and a number of other familiar names are historical figures rather than theorists whose work continues to be applied to present-day problems. Their ideas, though once credible, have been replaced by newer knowledge developed through more sophisticated means, much as our field understands the importance of someone like Melvil Dewey to the origins of the field rather than to our contemporary practice. We need to relinquish our attachment to the guidance offered by dated theory and invest our energies in assessing what valid, contemporary information about adolescence means to those of us invested in serving teens in the twenty-first century.

Further, we need to avoid the logical fallacy of assuming that less maturity means less autonomy, respect, or service. No one has argued that teens need simpler materials or that they should be kept from having certain kinds of information because of their ongoing brain development. Every cognitive scientist whose work I have read argues that their findings mean teens need more support, guidance, and encouragement. Relationships with trusted adults who can teach, mentor, and coach teens when their confidence either fails or isn't warranted are mentioned repeatedly as critical to teens' best interests in informed discussions of how we should think about their needs as they mature. The nature of communication with teens at this time is tremendously important, so ensuring that staff are practiced in firm but nonjudgmental messages as well as supportive ones is paramount to teens' perceptions of libraries as helpful places. Developing additional, institutional strategies for serving in supporting roles during younger library users' growth and change would be another way of responding to newer findings about the teen brain.

What emerges from the interdisciplinary research is that teens' decision-making abilities will be taking shape during their time in young adult departments and for years afterward. While ALA's Free Access to Libraries for Minors policy unequivocally disallows librarians to "predict what resources will best fulfill the needs and interests of any individual user based on a single criterion such as chronological age, educational level, literacy skills, or legal emancipation," a review of the research literature reveals that "most elements of cognitive development show a trajectory that follows age and experience."[61] In other words, while there are variations in youths' situations, the very criteria that ALA policy rejects as determinants of appropriateness are regarded by others as indicators of skills and abilities. Figuring out how to have conversations across disciplines, despite these differences, matters as we direct our attention to collaboration and community engagement. If we know that young people need guidance in order to achieve optimal outcomes and we cannot take on parental roles, then we should consider ways to promote, as our statements on library use by minors advise, our interest in parents' guidance of "their own children's use of the library and its resources and services." The best ways to serve young people may involve acknowledging their relationships with others, recognizing their needs as well as their rights.

FOR FURTHER READING

BrainFacts.org. "Neuromyths." www.brainfacts.org/neuromyths/.
    Assertions about how we use—or don't use—our brains abound. A series of short explanations rebuts popular misconstructions of brain science, including the idea that personality and aptitude reflect the use of a particular side of the brain, the contention that we only use 10 percent of our brains, and fearmongering about the use of drugs and alcohol. References and resources for further reading are included.

Jensen, Frances E., with Amy Ellis Nutt. *The Teenage Brain:*
A Neuroscientist's Survival Guide to Raising Adolescents and
Young Adults. New York: Harper Collins, 2015.

> Scientist and mother Frances Jensen turned her attention to recent
> cognitive science on adolescent development as her sons entered
> their teens. Importantly, she intends the book for "teenagers
> themselves" as well as "people helping to raise adolescents" (n.p.).
> The result of her explorations and her parenting is a substantive
> though readable volume that explains what happens inside teens'
> heads as they transition toward adulthood. Her work intends to
> prove that "no matter the evidence of their peculiar, sometimes
> infuriating behavior, teenagers are not irrational" (105). By ex-
> plaining how the teen brain is developing, she hopes to make
> connected, caring relationships between parents and adolescents
> less prone to strife. A series of short, related talks are available
> via YouTube at www.youtube.com/playlist?list=PLA20F6C776B
> CAFF4B.

Spinks, Sarah. "Adolescent Brains Are Works in Progress."
Frontline: Inside the Teenage Brain, 2002. www.pbs.org/wgbh/
pages/frontline/shows/teenbrain/work/adolescent.html.

> Online material developed in conjunction with the pioneering
> *Frontline* documentary on adolescent brain research has been
> maintained to address basic questions by balancing science
> with scrutiny of the implications and the limitations of this still-
> developing area of research.

Weinberger, Daniel R., Brita Elvevag, and Jay N. Giedd. *The*
Adolescent Brain: A Work in Progress. Washington, DC:
National Campaign to Prevent Teen Pregnancy, 2005.

> This 36-page white paper offers an explanation of how teen brain
> development affects decision-making capabilities involved in risk-
> taking behaviors. The authors of this paper acknowledge concerns
> about the potential for findings to have negative repercussions on
> teens' rights but counter that teens are not disempowered by this
> research. "No one," writes National Campaign to Prevent Teen
> Pregnancy then-director Sarah S. Brown in her introduction to

this paper, "should turn away from new research findings just because they might modify our thinking."

Young Adult Development Project. "Brain Changes." MIT. http://hrweb.mit.edu/worklife/youngadult/brain.html.
This site offers an overview of brain anatomy and short summaries of core changes in each region during adolescence. This page on the brain is part of a cluster that presents perspectives on contemporary issues in adolescent development. A bibliography of more than five hundred resources can be downloaded from the site.

NOTES

1. Jay Giedd, "What Goes on in the Adolescent Brain?" video, National Institute of Mental Health, May 8, 2015, www.nimh.nih.gov/health/topics/child-and-adolescent-mental-health/index.shtml (video no longer on website). Related talks: National Institute of Mental Health, "Development of the Young Brain," YouTube video, May 2, 2011, www.nimh.nih.gov/news/media/2011/giedd.shtml; UNSWTV, "Inside the adolescent brain—Talking Point with Dr Jay Giedd," YouTube video, September 20, 2012, www.youtube.com/watch?v=2nEBVtPmeCQ; Brain & Behavior Research Foundation, "The Teen Brain: Insights from Neuroimaging," YouTube video, January 27, 2014, www.youtube.com/watch?v=dsmXrqHLwto.

2. "Alabama Lawyer Seeks to Remind School-Based Police That Students Are Still Children," *PBS NewsHour,* August 8, 2016, www.pbs.org/newshour/bb/alabama-lawyer-seeks-remind-school-based-police-students-still-children.

3. Laurence Steinberg, *Age of Opportunity: Lessons from the New Science of Adolescence* (New York: Houghton Mifflin, 2014), 5.

4. Ibid., 4.

5. The Archimedes Palimpsest, http://archimedespalimpsest.org/images/kaltoon/. I love it, and you will too.

6. Barbara Strauch, *The Primal Teen: What the New Discoveries about the Teenage Brain Tell Us about Our Kids* (New York: Doubleday, 2003), 65.

7. Frances E. Jensen with Amy Ellis Nutt, *The Teenage Brain: A Neuroscientist's Survival Guide to Raising Adolescents and Young Adults* (New York: Harper Collins, 2015), 34–35, 36.

8. "Brain Backgrounders," Society for Neuroscience, http://apu.sfn.org (site discontinued).

9. Jay Giedd, interview, *Frontline: Inside the Teenage Brain,* 2002, www.pbs.org/wgbh/pages/frontline/shows/teenbrain/interviews/giedd.html.

10. Strauch, *The Primal Teen,* 43.

11. "Brain Basics," BrainFacts.org, 2016, www.brainfacts.org.

12. Strauch, *The Primal Teen,* 52–53.

13. Jensen and Nutt, *The Teenage Brain,* 37.

14. A. Rae Simpson, "Brain Changes," MIT Young Adult Development Project, 2008, http://hrweb.mit.edu/worklife/youngadult/brain.html.

15. Steinberg, *Age of Opportunity,* 10.

16. Jami Jones, "Teens Will Be Teens: The Latest Brain Research Has a Lot to Say about Adolescent Behavior," *School Library Journal* 51, no. 1 (January 2005): 37.

17. Jensen and Nutt, *The Teenage Brain,* 40.

18. "What Is Neuroscience?" Society for Neuroscience, http://apu.sfn.org/index.cfm?pagename=whatIsNeuroscience (site discontinued). See also "About Neuroscience," Society for Neuroscience, www.sfn.org/about/about-neuroscience, and "History of SfN," Society for Neuroscience, www.sfn.org/about/history-of-sfn.

19. Jensen and Nutt, *The Teenage Brain,* 4.

20. Beatriz Luna and John A. Sweeney, "The Emergence of Collaborative Brain Function: fMRI Studies of the Development of Response Inhibition," in *Adolescent Brain Development: Vulnerabilities and Opportunities,* ed. Ronald E. Dahl and Linda Patia Spear, Annals of the New York Academy of Sciences 1021 (New York: New York Academy of Sciences, 2004).

21. Misia Landau, "Deciphering the Adolescent Brain," *Focus: News from Harvard Medical, Dental, and Public Health Schools,* April 21, 2000.

22. Sarah Spinks, "Adolescent Brains Are Works in Progress," *Frontline: Inside the Teenage Brain,* 2002, www.pbs.org/wgbh/pages/frontline/shows/teenbrain/work/adolescent.html.

23. Jensen and Nutt, *The Teenage Brain,* 40.

24. Spinks, *Adolescent Brains Are Works in Progress.*

25. Giedd, interview, *Frontline;* Bryan Stevenson, Just Mercy (New York: Spiegel and Grau, 2015).

26. Ronald E. Dahl, "Adolescent Brain Development: A Period of Vulnerabilities and Opportunities," keynote address, in *Adolescent Brain Development: Vulnerabilities and Opportunities,* ed. Ronald E. Dahl and

Linda Patia Spear, Annals of the New York Academy of Sciences 1021 (New York: New York Academy of Sciences, 2004).

27. *Frontline: Inside the Teenage Brain,* DVD (2002; PBS Video, 2004).

28. Strauch, *The Primal Teen,* 207.

29. Jay Giedd, interview by Eleanor Imster, "Studying Teens from the Inside Out," *Earth and Sky* (site discontinued).

30. Steinberg, Age of Opportunity, 19, 21.

31. Dahl, "Adolescent Brain Development," 6.

32. Strauch, *The Primal Teen,* 44.

33. Giedd, interview, *Earth and Sky.*

34. Giedd, interview, *Frontline.*

35. Strauch, *The Primal Teen,* 65.

36. Dahl, "Adolescent Brain Development," 19.

37. Jensen and Nutt, *The Teenage Brain,* 105–6.

38. Dahl, "Adolescent Brain Development," 19.

39. Jensen and Nutt, *The Teenage Brain,* 292.

40. Ibid., 290.

41. Landau, "Deciphering the Adolescent Brain."

42. Cathy De Rosa et al., *College Students' Perceptions of Libraries and Information Resources* (Dublin, OH: OCLC, 2006), 5–4, www.oclc.org/reports/pdfs/studentperceptions.pdf.

43. Ibid., 4–9.

44. Valerie Strauss, "Schools Waking Up to Teens' Unique Sleep Needs," *Washington Post,* January 10, 2006, www.washingtonpost.com/wp-dyn/content/article/2006/01/09/AR2006010901561.html.

45. *Frontline: Inside the Teenage Brain.*

46. Strauch, *The Primal Teen,* 159.

47. *Frontline: Inside the Teenage Brain.*

48. Jensen and Nutt, *The Teenage Brain,* 21, 22.

49. Ronald E. Dahl and Ahmad R. Hariri, "Lessons from G. Stanley Hall: Conducting New Research in Biological Sciences to the Study of Adolescent Development," *Journal of Research on Adolescence* 15, no. 4 (November 2005): 371, 372.

50. Ronald Dahl in discussion with the author, November 2006.

51. Cindy Welch, "Teen Volunteers to the Rescue!" in *How to Thrive as a Solo Librarian,* ed. Carol Smallwood and Melissa J. Clapp (Lanham, MD: Scarecrow Press, 2012), 69–82.

52. Terry McCarthy, "Getting Inside Your Head," *Time,* October 24, 2005, 97.

53. Wendy Melillo, "Inside the Consumer Mind: What Neuroscience Can Tell Us about Marketing," *Adweek,* January 16, 2006, www.adweek.com/news/advertising/inside-consumer-mind-83549.

54. See, e.g., Public Citizen's Commercial Alert's web page at http://archive.commercialalert.org/issues/culture/neuromarketing.

55. Giedd, interview, *Earth and Sky.*

56. Margaret Talbot, "The Baby Brain: What Infants' Brains Tell Us about Our Own," *New Yorker,* September 4, 2006: 90–101.

57. Daniel R. Weinberger, Brita Elvevag, and Jay N. Giedd, *The Adolescent Brain: A Work in Progress* (Washington, DC: National Campaign to Prevent Teen Pregnancy, 2005), 19.

58. Dahl, "Adolescent Brain Development," 20.

59. Ibid., 2.

60. Weinberger et al., *The Adolescent Brain,* 19.

61. Office for Intellectual Freedom of the American Library Association, comp., "Free Access to Libraries for Minors: An Interpretation of the Library Bill of Rights," in *Intellectual Freedom Manual,* 7th ed. (Chicago: American Library Association, 2006), 152, 153; Dahl, "Adolescent Brain Development," 15.

Five

Mediating
the World

The idea that young people are distinctively attuned to technology is long-standing, and questions about the implications are pervasive. One recent example can be found in Robert MacFarlane's protest against replacing terms describing the natural world with words for technology in the revised *Oxford Junior Dictionary*. Instead of *acorn*, there is *attachment*; instead of *buttercup*, there is *blog*; instead of *mistletoe*, there is *MP3 player*, and so on. Editors claimed that words for plants, birds, and animals no longer express "the consensus experience" of young people but new technology does.[1] (Neither disputant considers, however, what might spur young readers to opt for a hefty dictionary rather than *Wikipedia* or a Google search.) MacFarlane and others who take up the topic of teens and technology are concerned with the ways media influence our understanding and interactions. Given the changing and proliferating media now available, study of the uses and the effects of content and devices prevails in interdisciplinary research, offering librarians context for assessing the resources and services they offer to teens.

Librarians have worried about the role of technology and reading in young people's lives since the first years of the profession, and some older contentions can seem remarkably contemporary, if conservative. In 1969 a midwestern librarian argued that media encroached on the terrain of the book, expressing concern about young people's reliance on fragmented information in varying formats. Youth were inundated with media products, she observed:

> It is conceivable that in today's world of mass media information services, the electronic classroom—where we find the pursuit of multi-sensory education—and the media center replacing the school library, that the term BOOK needs to be defined. As book publishers are being purchased by the large electronic industries, they find their materials—what they had recently termed books—assume the character of filmstrips, tapes, recordings, single-concept loop films, even fragmented into transparencies. The child is no longer instructed by the teacher to go to the library to find a book about birds. The child is told to go to the media center and find ADDITIONAL INFORMATION about birds. This could be a recording of bird songs, a set of transparencies with overlays showing perhaps even a stuffed bird and a real nest that he has discovered on the shelf of realia.[2]

These words may strike us as both nostalgic and—barring their references to obsolete technologies—remarkably prescient, an evocation of long ago and an articulation of professional angst that some still feel today.

The tug of technology and whether it enhances or detracts from young people's capabilities may be an old theme, but in the twenty-first century many fields see qualitative and quantitative differences in young people's media use then and now.[3] For years, studies have found that U.S. teens log an impressive number of hours listening to music, chatting via cell phones, and watching television—perhaps even at the same time. The most recent figures indicate an average of nine hours of use each day. In 2012 nearly all teens reported watching at least some television each day, but today cell phones are in the lead and now create access to a variety of content, whether videos or interactions with peers.[4] Although some researchers acknowledge difficulties and nuances in creating large-scale assessments of teens' media-related activities, particularly online, no one disputes that technology and the media it makes available loom large in teens' lives.[5] Kaiser Family Foundation researcher Victoria Rideout stated, "These kids are spending the equivalent of a full-time work week using media, plus overtime. Anything that takes up that much space in their lives certainly deserves our full attention."[6]

The abundance of media available to teens is another substantial theme. The "rapidly changing media landscape" differs from the not-too-distant past, when modern electronic media made real inroads into consumers' lives:

> Whereas children in the 1950s had at most five or six television channels to choose from, a handful of local radio stations that played their kind of music, and one or two movie theaters within walking or driving distance, today's youth can select from hundreds of media sources literally all over the world. The sheer volume of content available is mind boggling, and . . . thanks to digital technology, the fidelity of the sights and sounds that travel with them in cars, on bikes or skateboards, and on airplanes, can be startling.[7]

Researcher Frances Jensen has summarized the facts, saying, "Today's teenagers and twenty-somethings make up the first generation of young people exposed to such a breathtaking number of electronic distractions."[8] Other researchers have described the effects more conclusively. Jay Giedd has observed that the media expands "the world of peers" so that the individuals who influence and respond to a teen's decisions are no longer limited to a neighborhood or a school; others have observed that the expanded networks of online friends mean parents no longer know the people their teens spend time with.[9] Jane Brown's research leads her to characterize the media as a "super peer" that makes the behaviors and attitudes of teen characters appealing and influential as teens gain autonomy.[10]

Many authors map the lives of young people against time lines of technological change.[11] Descriptions of younger library users as digital natives are common, although the label emerged from an opinion piece rather than research.[12] The Beloit College Mindset List routinely notes technologies that have become obsolete or existed for the entirety of an eighteen-year-old's life, as in the "Class of 2019 List" which reminds faculty that students entering college in 2016 have never known a world without Wi-Fi or Google and regard e-mail as a slightly stodgy, formal mode of communication.[13] The message of this kind of commentary is that the young are very different from you and me by virtue of their side-by-side development with newer information and communication technologies, yet many questions about teens and technology are far from settled.

We routinely witness competing claims about technology, hearing one day that *Everything Bad Is Good for You* and the next "How Computers Make Our Kids Stupid."[14] The issues are considerably more complex than these black-and-white stances suggest, as shown by research taking place outside of LIS. Even as library journals warn professionals that they "can't be information experts if they don't have basic tech skills" and libraries circulate video games, researchers renew their efforts to assess teens' use of new and old technologies.[15] Their findings are essential to distinguishing between warnings worth heeding and ill-informed complaints about a younger generation's behavior, and they support librarians' abilities to defend their service plans to critical audiences. That ongoing, interdisciplinary work examines a wide array of media-related topics, including print versus digital reading, cell phone use and so-called Internet addiction, multitasking, online fan communities, and video games.

READING ON THE PAGE, SOCIALIZING ON SCREEN

What we know about teens as readers comes from varied sources. There are scholarly works that attempt to fathom the cultural aspects of literacy and what happens to our brains when we read, and there are market studies that refute popular perceptions of teens as oriented to digital domains. Researchers have begun to demonstrate that allegiance to print isn't simply old-fashioned; many teens remain convinced of the value of print, and there are indications that it aids certain types of cognitive activity.[16] Still there are clear indicators that, regardless of the fact that print is not passé for teens, screen time figures prominently in their social lives. Indeed, a dimension of reading that marketers have attempted to exploit and researchers are beginning to understand is that teens' reading has a social, interactive, online dimension.[17] Numerous researchers and experts offer us ways to think about these dynamics.

When e-readers emerged anew in 2009, young readers figured prominently in the anticipated market for the devices. Newspaper headlines highlighted teens' interest in screen-based reading, and new predictions about the resulting demise of the book followed. Since then, the trends have moderated. Surveys show that most teens prefer print books, particularly for studying, and analysts draw attention to the fact that e-book sales, besides leveling off in recent years, still constitute a small percentage of the overall book market.[18] Purchasing patterns are indicators that despite teens' attachment to their smartphones, they have not abandoned books. Naomi S. Baron, author of *Words Onscreen: The Fate of Reading in a Digital World*, documented college students' conviction that print reading matter enhances their concentration and focus. Others have shown that teens who read *Harry Potter* demonstrated stronger empathy and less prejudice, suggesting social as well as cognitive gains accrue from long-form reading.[19]

University researchers want to understand teens' reading behaviors at a deeper level, but that endeavor will take years. They believe that we are in an era of change, in which conclusions about how or whether technology affects students' learning are as yet limited. Maryanne Wolf, author of *Proust and the Squid: The Story and Science of the Reading Brain*, has argued that "'the reading brain is literally molting under everyone's fingertips.'"[20] Some find less difference in print and screen-based reading comprehension, though few trust that these results are conclusive. As Baron told *The Chronicle of Higher Education,* "Researchers cannot rely on students' immediate recall of what they just read, as most studies have done so far. How that text might have shifted their thinking, influenced their analysis, fostered their emotional growth, or nested in their brains for years are all variables to consider that are not yet easily measurable."[21]

Multiple people drive our attention not so much to media as to what it conveys, focusing on stories. One expert who sees teens' devotion to media, whether books, television, or fan fiction, in positive terms, explains young people's interest: "Story is powerful," Kathleen Smith states, and she goes on to describe particular mechanisms in the brain that respond to it.[22] Stress, she observes, generates a more intense response to dopamine, which "helps control the brain's reward and pleasure centers."[23] Smith believes that the rewards of stories' familiar characters and satisfying endings, regardless of medium, offer us a way to feel good when other things in life cause anxiety and tension. She warns her readers that real-life changes often don't happen the way we see them on-screen and that to solve problems we'll probably have to take different steps than our favorite character.

Still, Smith doesn't chastise fans for deep involvement with stories, but she does discuss how to use time, energy, and all-important releases productively. Obsessive engagement with media, she contends, can create its own sort of stress, and young adults need to find balance in this dimension of their lives. "These behaviors may feel rewarding in the moment," she acknowledges, "but they are not the self-care you need." How we interact with others online is another dimension of fan culture, and Smith urges teens to trade reflection and mindfulness over instantaneous reaction:

> Social media culture does not lend itself to real reflection. The itch of the fingers to tweet a complaint or text your fury can switch off the ability to be thoughtful. . . . Emotionally intelligent humans hit the pause button to gauge a situation with their prefrontal cortex. But if you're always racing to be the first one to have a hilariously ragey comment on the Internet, then you'll just get wound up tighter and tighter.[24]

Her honest and frank look at how media and mind interact explains why teens make some of the choices they do and offers ways to think about altering less desirable media-inflected behaviors. Interestingly, she says that keeping behavioral goals to ourselves is important to enhancing the odds of successful change: "Science tells us . . . yakking about our intentions boosts our self-esteem enough that we don't feel like we have to do anything else."[25] We may find that teens most readily accept her insights if discovered on their own or through a trusted advisor rather than delivered as a lecture.

Another researcher also articulates strong reasons for teens' online activities, noting that the technologies that were developed for pragmatic purposes now play roles in normal, long-standing behavior. In *It's Complicated*, danah boyd reminds us that "the importance of friends in social and moral development is well documented. But the fears that surround teens' use of social media overlook this fundamental desire for social connection."[26] Four aspects of online communication shift perceptions of the dynamic, boyd argues. She observes that social-media sites are designed to create *persistence*, or the "durability of online expression;" *visibility* to a "potential audience;" *spreadability*, or means of sharing; and *searchability*, the "ability to find content."[27] These four features change the way teens' use of a site or platform is construed, giving it a different valence than socializing the way it has played out historically. Despite this, she believes "social media . . . is a release valve, allowing youth to reclaim meaningful sociality as a tool for managing the pressures and limitations around them."[28] Not everyone is as sanguine about teens' online socializing, but boyd's words offer a useful reminder about what motivates teens to connect.

Sherry Turkle is one researcher who raises questions about teens' reliance on technology. At the Public Library Association 2016 Conference, she told librarians, "Technology is implicated in an assault on empathy," referring to measurable declines in feeling for others as reflected in tests on college campuses. It's not just their interactions with others that are challenged by technology; Turkle argues that it lowers teens' resilience too. One teen told her, "I'd rather text than talk," a remark she sees as symptomatic of a withdrawal from the open-ended dynamics of conversation, which involve risk and vulnerability. "Human relationships are rich, and they are messy, and we try to clean them up with technology," she said. Yet there is a difference between a transaction and a relationship, Turkle explained, and real-time exchanges are essential to the latter.[29]

She doesn't demonize devices in our daily lives or advocate that we give up our cell phones entirely, congruent with other researchers who have observed, "Cellular telephones have become firmly entrenched in contemporary American society as a critical medium through which interpersonal connectedness is maintained." Particularly for younger teens, cell phones facilitate the "development of both autonomy and connection." Multiple studies show that parents are a primary contact for teens. Parents talk to the teens via cell phone about four times a day and may constitute one-third of a teen's texts.[30] Acknowledging the reality of the omnipresent cell phone, she urges a more mindful, reflective use, whether it's how they fill our solitary moments or social ones. "You need the capacity to be alone," to engage in "uni-tasking" and long-form reading, Turkle urged. The resulting self-reflection supports a person's capacity for interaction. Turkle explained that the lulls and the tedium of waiting in line, which we try to fill with quick messages or Facebook posts, can be downtime that our brains need; the brain is active, processing events and messages, once no longer actively navigating those experiences via cell phone. Turkle cites research showing it's not just teens who live this way; a 2015 survey saw 89 percent of Americans acknowledge using their phones during a recent conversation, with most admitting that it affected the quality of the exchange. In encouraging teens not to turn to their phones unthinkingly, Turkle believes we support their development of attributes like creativity, intimacy, or caring.[31] She is not alone. Cognitive scientist Jensen, who understands teens' reliance on cell phones in part because of the opportunity to observe her own sons' adolescence, concurs in saying that people need time away from technology. She indicates that adults must model these behaviors, instead of just expecting teens to go without checking for texts from time to time: "There is no turning back from the digital world we all live in, but we can turn away—if even for a few minutes or hours a day—and the earlier we start doing this with our kids, the better." Her advice is to "approach the problem not as something your teen is being punished for but as something he or she needs help with in order to stay balanced, well rounded, and less isolated."[32]

These experts recognize that we use technology and the stories we share through it to create comfort and connections in our lives, though they regard what happens online differently. They believe that teens can benefit from the relationships and communication facilitated by it. While boyd views social-media platforms as a release from the structures that prevail elsewhere in adolescents' lives, other specialists see a need to refrain from using devices and encourage teens—and the rest of us—to turn to books and each other from time to time.

INTERACTIONS

Interactivity is one aspect of new technology that generates attention from users, creators, reporters, and scholars alike. A somewhat fluid concept, *interactivity* refers to the ways a user engages with technology, whether by being able to shape a narrative and manipulate content or, from some perspectives, simply by paying nuanced attention to the ins and outs of twisting plots. VidCon and Vlogbrothers cocreator Hank Green has described us as living in "the first age of the social internet," a time when "share-ability is king."[33] Interactivity may refer to a range of actions, from participating in an online conversation in a chat room to liking a Facebook post or retweeting. It is further characterized by the potential to influence others outside the immediate exchange, as shown by a study that found teens respond and react more strongly to Facebook posts they believe have a higher number of peer-generated "likes."[34] As online platforms develop, interactivity manifests in new ways. This facet of electronic media is not entirely new, given early efforts to encourage television viewers' reactions to on-screen content.[35] Nonetheless, it is seen as a defining characteristic of technological change. In education circles, interactivity is also regarded as an aspect of play that builds skills, which legitimizes young people's use of technologies.

Interactivity has both benefits and drawbacks. Advocates contend that technology helps tweens and teens develop a new and more sophisticated kind of knowledge. Technology is not just a tool from this perspective, but a revolutionary force that requires us to reconceptualize learning. Its potential also includes facilitating connections with others, regardless of geographic location. Online communities are diverse in their cultures and purposes but generally are understood as "groups of people who interact in virtual environments with a purpose, following certain norms, and supported by technology."[36] Connecting with authors, YouTube creators, and other performers are increasingly normal parts of teen life. As Sarah Urist Green, creator of the Art Assignment, once told the *New Yorker,* "Being a fan is so much a part of young life now."[37] While researchers believe that continued scrutiny of these communities eventually will yield all sorts of information, including "how individuals engage with media and for what reasons," studies of predominantly teen-populated online communities are as yet limited.[38] Some of the research to date observes feelings of connection and validation among participants.

Potentially detrimental media effects stem from the history of how people have reacted to developments in the technology that makes media available. For decades people have wondered whether media might harm young audiences. Ellen Wartella and Byron Reeves observed, "With the development of each modern means of storytelling—books, newspapers, movies, radio, comics and television—social debates regarding their effects have recurred."[39] These perceived threats have been both physical, when it was thought sitting too close to a television might hurt one's eyes, and psychological, as reflected by ongoing attention to the impact of on-screen violence. Although the concept of physical harm might seem old-fashioned, at least one very recent research study warns about hearing loss caused by excessive device volume, and a cell phone manufacturer recalled a particular model of phone following bans by U.S. airlines because the phone battery was prone to explosion.[40]

One issue often highlighted in discussions of young people's use of interactive technologies is so-called addiction, whether to the Internet or to their cell phones. It is important to be aware that the concept arose in 1995 as satire by a psychologist who wanted to make a point about diagnostic criteria and language in contemporary society.[41] Jensen, who is among the experts who call our attention to Internet addiction's lack of status as a disorder recognized by professionals, explains teens' behavior this way: "Technology is another opportunity for novelty seeking, and because the brain of a teenager is so easy to stimulate, all it takes is the latest digital toy to tease it into distraction."[42]

Other concerns about the latest technology focus on the potential for people to harm each other through the exchanges it makes possible. Wartella and Nancy Jennings explain, "The introduction of computer technology into children's lives parallels the introduction of previous waves of new media and technology throughout the past century. . . . But the interactivity that is the hallmark of children's use of new media enables both greatly enriched learning as well as increased risk of harm."[43] The potential for adult strangers to prey on young people online or for the anonymity afforded by the Internet to allow peer harassment are among the more prominent concerns today.

Whereas boyd characterizes much teen online interaction as disturbing only when taken out of context, others see genuinely threatening and alarming misconduct in online venues popular with teens. Patricia Greenfield, who leads the Children's Digital Media Center at UCLA, has described a scenario in which she anonymously entered a teen chat room, only to find her persona there propositioned and subjected to abusive language. Some teens behave this way in spaces where their identity is hidden from their peers and their conduct is unseen by adults, according to the Brookings Institute, which concluded that it is difficult to determine how widespread cyberbullying is because of varying definitions and reporting systems.[44] "Many parents are quite unaware of the kind of social and cultural worlds young people are creating online," Greenfield writes. "The nature and norms of these cultures can be very much influenced by adult rules, regulations, & participatory monitoring."[45] She is not alone in observing that "none of the developmental issues raised is unique to the Internet."

Many entities call for policy and education to combat the problems resulting from online interactions gone wrong, and librarians are well positioned to fulfill these needs. Creating usage guidelines for in-library computing centers and offering programs that inform parents and teens about strategies for protecting privacy and personal dignity are two clear ways to respond to teens' inclinations and the realities of the environment. Green, who loves the exchange of ideas taking place online and the communities that form around it, has also said, "the internet has become a less kind place."[46] Enabling teens to enjoy its resources and the interactions it makes possible, as well as teaching them how to react in the event of targeted unkindness, is critical. Teens should learn the ethics and safeguards that will allow them to avoid being drawn into threatening exchanges. Research indicates there is a need for education that "takes different risk profiles into account" rather than the "'one-size-fits-all' type of messaging [that] has sometimes dominated." There has also been a call for evidence to inform the messages used in these information sessions.[47] Librarians' pursuit of this type of information, then, would be broadly beneficial and would open communication with others who want to understand teens' social exchanges.

MUCH ADO ABOUT MULTITASKING

Recent surveys indicate that one factor contributing to the intense hours of tweens' and teens' media use is their predilection for using multiple media at the same time. This behavior has been given the label *multitasking,* or trying "to perform two tasks simultaneously, switch from one task to another, or perform two or more tasks in rapid succession."[48] Some researchers prefer the term *media multi-tasking.* They observe that the nature of multitasking may be cognitively varied, as "some combinations like doing homework with background media . . . have both tasks going on all the time. Others, like reading and instant messaging, require you to switch back and forth." Those differences are important to outcomes.[49] The activity is performed by a small but substantial number of teens, according to communications researchers.[50]

This behavior has generated significant media and scholarly attention. In the recent past, authoritative commentators have argued that teens' manipulation of multiple forms of technology is simply normal, twenty-first-century adolescent behavior.[51] Since then, however, most researchers who have revisited the question of whether multitasking is an effective way of managing time and tasks have concluded that it is not, though some have questioned the evaluative criteria. A survey of the extant literature observes that one motivation for multitasking, "to make less pleasant tasks more pleasant," has been ignored by researchers and suggests assessment of "the extent to which it changes the multitaskers' emotional state and satisfaction."[52] Nonetheless, this evaluation of the extant research indicates that memory is routinely impaired by multitasking.

Some negative assessments are based on observations of brain activity. Russell Poldrack, an associate professor of psychology at UCLA, explains the problem (and the obvious solution) this way:

> Multi-tasking adversely affects how you learn. . . . Even if you learn while multi-tasking, that learning is less flexible and more specialized, so you cannot retrieve the information as easily. The best thing you can do to improve your memory is to pay attention to the things you want to remember. When distractions force you to pay less attention to what you are doing, you don't learn as well as if you had paid full attention.[53]

Over time, scientists have seen that "the quality of one's output and the depth of thought deteriorate as one attends to ever more tasks."[54]

Such findings suggest that librarians who love books and want to encourage young people to lose themselves in a favorite title aren't simply nostalgic; they are interested in a necessary, though less flashy, aspect of adolescent development. While there is an increasing amount of professional writing that promotes electronic activities to encourage teens' use of libraries, less is being said about the importance of maintaining spaces that facilitate attention and concentration for in-depth reading. Even as we endeavor to welcome teens by accepting noise and promoting video games at the library, we should maintain places where adolescents as well as adults are welcome to unplug from the multimedia-driven world. Encouraging young people to read books, it seems, is indeed a necessary counterpoint to facilitating their ready use of technology.

COMING TO TERMS WITH VIDEO GAMES

In the late twentieth century, we saw researchers and policy makers raise questions about the effects of violence portrayed on television and in video games. Researchers hesitated to conclude that young people were desensitized to violence or more prone to act out after viewing on-screen violence, seeing the association as overly simplistic. More recently, however, scholars have begun to temper these judgments, while youth librarians have begun to appreciate the ability of popular materials such as video games to draw young people to libraries. Our professional literature promotes gaming, promising that it educates, bridges the digital divide, and has patrons returning to libraries and borrowing books while there.[55] Librarians who pursue this increasingly popular direction of service should understand the questions raised by those outside our field.

There is no denying that contemporary video games are popular and compelling. At present, there are some 145 million people who play video games, whether via home consoles or online, in the United States. Of these, a mere 18 percent are under the age of eighteen. Statistics from 2010 indicated that the average player is active in the game world for twenty-two hours a week.[56]

Such figures might appear to support those who contend that video games are addictive. Most experts, however, attribute teens' passionate investment in these games to aspects of adolescent brain development associated with reward-seeking and risk-taking behaviors rather than to any genuinely addictive behavior. Likewise, detractors who argue teens lose control of their playing behavior and perform less successfully in school than their nonplaying peers are making claims not supported by empirical research. There are those, including academic researchers, who argue that games can support learning and serve good ends.

One small area of the video-game market comprises health-oriented games designed to educate young people about their health conditions and encourage their adherence to treatment regimens when ill, but they are not the only ones with the ability to boost young people's knowledge or change their behavior. No bland, moralistic fare here—one game developer referred to the products under development at his organization as "stealth learning" tools and recognized that "the things that happen inside the game don't stay in the game; they get in your head, and they change the way you approach the world."[57] One recent study has shown that younger students who played a particular video game fared better on school tests than nonplaying peers.[58] Others have described indirect health effects, such as the minimizing of young patients' fears and discomfort when they are allowed to play games during medical treatment.[59]

The potential for games to have positive effects is demonstrable through recent research, albeit contentious in some intellectual circles. There are indications that some games may induce players to embrace desirable attributes, like citizenship and activism, with the U.S. State Department among the entities encouraging game development in the interest of improving "America's reputation abroad."[60] For games to work as learning tools, though, educational play must have the same dramatic and visual appeal as the most popular commercial games, leading a number of prominent universities to become involved in developing games intended "to create learning simulations," whether present-day or historical.[61] More broadly, even those who articulate concerns about excessive video-game use acknowledge positive effects of play. The Media Awareness Network advises parents that children can realize a number of benefits by playing video games. They experience

- a fun and social form of entertainment
- teamwork and cooperation when games are played with others
- increased comfort with technology
- improved self-confidence and self-esteem

- increases in reading, math, and problem-solving skills and eye-hand coordination and fine motor skills[62]

Other sources also testify to these effects, and the library literature broadly asserts this sort of skill development.[63] We should see this research as urging librarians to seek out games with the potential to contribute to such positive effects on young people's skills, which often happens through collaborative play.

Drawing on the research of Jane McGonigal, Crash Course Games host Andre Meadows has urged viewers to understand that "games can be a force for good in the world."[64] Elsewhere, James Paul Gee has encouraged us to see video games as a cultural domain that requires interactive, evaluative knowledge. In other words, these games are a genre of their own, with rules and vocabulary like any other field or area of learning. While Gee doesn't consider gaming to be uniformly positive, he focuses on the activity's potential to compel attention and capture the imagination.[65] Apologists for video games talk about this medium's evocative nature and its cultural context. Gee, for example, has called video games a "powerful device" whose allure could be used "for both good and evil." He is not alone in praising games as a means of learning and experimentation with new ideas or skills, much as books have been noted as means of grappling with ideas outside one's immediate experience. Even PBS tells parents that "skill is required to use the controls; elaborate rules must be understood and mastered; and children this age have a growing interest in exploring the world and their place in it."[66]

The demonstrable issues with some video games, as well as their redeeming aspects, are ones youth services librarians should understand and respond to as they consider collection development and programming options. Often, these issues revolve around violence. Violence in video games, according to Gee, is controversial but in some cases can be understood as transformative, a temporary condition that will lead to more positive encounters.[67] Some librarians also promote doubts about the potentially negative consequences of video-game violence. One forceful defense of video-game violence characterized gaming's opponents as simply repeating old arguments:

"Video faced the same backlash in the 80s, music did in the 50s when Elvis shaked [*sic*] his hips. Now we think of it as laughable. I am fairly confident that this vilification of video games will be looked at in the same way in 20 years when the policy makers have grown up with video games as much as 30 year olds."[68] It is precisely these matters that researchers in a number of fields have been studying, looking at how young people behave in the real world after becoming acculturated to virtual ones. Critiques of game-world violence are being made not by old-fashioned individuals who think that young people should be reading the classics but by experienced scholars, many of whom are parents themselves.

Librarians should be aware that many recent, credible studies reject Gee's idealistic take on violent game content and indicate that industry defenses like the one above are patently untrue. An increasing number of researchers express the conviction that participatory on-screen violence has real-life consequences, though few believe in a linear, causal relationship between video games and violence. Instead, they contend that young players of violent games tend to show increased aggressiveness and antisocial behaviors in other, indirect ways.

Researchers have used a variety of methodologies to gain insights into the nature of interactions between gamers and video games. In particular, two studies have signaled that those who play violent video games do carry some of the attitudes and actions that enable their avatars to survive in the game world into the real world. This research concentrates on short-term rather than long-term effects. Games that create stories, an aspect sometimes lauded as educational, are considered to have stronger effects and to attract young players more intensely.[69] The result is that young people are more likely to have incorporated the ideas integral to their game experiences into their overall worldviews, making them more accepting of violence beyond the context of their games. In short, a game's narrative helps justify its characters' violent actions and reinforces a violent perspective, which creates the possibility that its effects will extend beyond the game.

Another study explored the potential for lasting effects by evaluating how teens' brains respond to different kinds of video games. Young people between the ages of thirteen and seventeen played either a popular violent video game or another fast-paced video game without violent content. According to news reports on the conference where this research was presented, "Those who played the violent video game showed more activation in the amygdala, which is involved in emotional arousal, and less activation in the prefrontal portions of the brain associated with control, focus, and concentration than the teens who played the nonviolent game."[70] In other words, playing the violent video game activated the teens' fight-or-flight responses. These states were observed not when the teens were actively playing the violent game but during different tasks that they were asked to complete after concluding their game sessions. Video imaging of players' brains contributed to researchers' conclusions that the emotional states developed during violent play don't end when the game is won, lost, or paused. The aggressive outlook can persist.

If our interest is in supporting positive youth development as well as attracting young people to libraries, serious attention to research findings on the negative effects of games becomes a necessary aspect of collection development. For librarians developing video-game collections, familiarity with actual game content is more important than awareness of enthusiastic reviews or ratings. Multiple sources indicate that simply because a game is industry rated as appropriate for teen players does not mean it is free of either violent or sexual content. Reviews of games done by individuals interested in youth development should play a part in determining that video games belong in library collections. Following interviews with a number of experts in this area, PBS editors advised parents to avoid purchasing first-person shooter games in which a young person "takes on the identity of a violent character," sometimes referred to simply as role-playing games.[71] Advocates for young people urge our attention to issues like racial and gender stereotyping, particularly when it comes to the depiction of female characters and ethnic minorities as victims. They have asked for the development and promotion of games with

African-American or female protagonists, and they reject scripts that reward violence. Librarians could consult published, research-informed evaluative criteria and draw their own conclusions after playing the games themselves.

Bandura and the Bobo Doll: Early Efforts at Showing How Media Matter

Where do contemporary ideas about young people's impressionable acquisition of ideas presented on-screen come from? The research of Albert Bandura, a noted psychologist whose work is integral to theories of social learning, is one source. In the early 1960s, Bandura and his associates conducted research on children and their reenactments of observed violence inflicted on a blow-up clown called Bobo.[72] Bandura believed, and demonstrated, that "observation is a powerful mechanism of learning."[73] His interest in different processes and effects of learning from modeled behavior resulted in experiments that refined scientific thought about how people learn, including the role of imagination. Bandura's framework of learning processes includes four subprocesses: *attention,* or the ability to determine important aspects of an observed behavior; *retention,* which has been described as representing the modeled activity "in symbolic form for later use" or the ability to derive generalizations from others' actions; *reproduction,* or converting the symbolic codes of memory into action once more; and *motive or incentive conditions* for doing so. "Observational learning is governed by these four subfunctions," Bandura has stated. "Children can acquire fairly complex patterns . . . simply by observation."[74]

The principle is ingenious in its clarity and power. Bandura noted that without abstract modeling, or the ability to extend the principles grasped from one observed encounter into new ones, learning would be extremely limited. Children's language learning is one example of how this takes place in the real world: rather than simply repeating what they hear, children also discern linguistic principles, like subject-verb order, to create new sentences that they've never heard. Psychologists like Bandura, however, have also been interested in how observation informs social actions, including those presented via media such as television and movies. His research linked observation to subsequent behavior, and he noted that positive as well as negative behaviors can be gained this way. Televised violence was a significant interest in some of his groundbreaking research.[75] ■

SEX, MEDIA, AND ADOLESCENT WELL-BEING

Researchers have long sought to understand whether electronic media, including downloaded music, affect young people's health and well-being. Influential studies have considered a range of effects, such as adolescents' decisions to smoke and to engage in other behaviors with health consequences, like sexual activity.[76] The results have led researchers from multiple fields to place an increased importance on ensuring teens' access to a variety of messages and media literacy concepts.

The sexual content of music will continue to be scrutinized following prominent studies that signal its effects on young people's ideas about sexuality. It has been shown, repeatedly, that popular music contains more sexual references than other media young people are exposed to each day.[77] One 2006 study that focused exclusively on music found that teens who listened to songs with sexually explicit lyrics became sexually active in higher proportions than teens who listened to music with less explicit content. The study tracked attitudes and actions across multiple years, seeking to account for music among the influences on teens' decision making.[78] The results of this study, though contested by individuals ranging from rap stars to fellow researchers, are congruent with other contemporary research. Researchers concluded, "The study found that the more time adolescents spend listening to music with sexually degrading lyrics, the more likely they are to initiate intercourse and other sexual activities. This holds true for boys and girls as well as for whites and nonwhites, even after accounting for a wide range of other personal and social factors associated with adolescent sexual behavior."[79]

When it comes to rap music, a small group of researchers has found preliminary psychophysiological evidence—data about emotional response based on measures like heart rate and muscle tension—that young people also may have other kinds of reactions to degrading, sexually charged remarks in the lyrics of some of the most popular songs. Interestingly, while young women reacted negatively to songs that depicted them as sex objects, young men did not show aversion to lyrics that characterized them in the same way. This information results from a small data set, and further work would be needed to clarify the findings and to determine whether they are characteristic of a broader group of young people.[80] Still, it suggests that adolescents may respond differently to popular music and that the differences may be attributable to gender. Young adult librarians who collect rap, hip-hop, and other popular music must know when the music they purchase for their collections contains misogynist and sexually explicit lyrics and when the music they acquire in the same genres has less charged language. It's not a matter of censorship but of appeal. If research results are any indication, popular songs and artists may not be uniformly desirable to teens of both sexes.

Studying music in this way is a relatively recent academic enterprise, but results to date indicate that the words teens encounter through entertainment outlets have potentially significant effects on their young lives. Findings about reactions to the sexual content of song lyrics underscore the challenge of developing collection policies that focus on music for younger listeners. Librarians serving teens need to understand these findings, which drive attention to the importance of incorporating multiple voices and perspectives in collections.

Recent investigations have brought both new techniques to the effort to understand links between media and life choices and calls for the improvement of adolescents' media literacy. Notably, researchers who are uncovering the connections between young adults' viewing habits and their real-life actions advocate media literacy to counteract the tendency of media to function "as a kind of super peer for young people, glamorizing and normalizing often unhealthy behavior." Researchers urge those who conduct media literacy educational programs, which must account for the multiple platforms that are significant in adolescents' lives, to

- help young people understand that "the media are in the business of selling them products and behaviors that often are not good for them"
- focus attention on aspects of how the media work, including "reality and representation"
- supplement these kinds of critical thinking skills with "positive extracurricular activities . . . that help youth build nurturing connections with peers . . . based on young people's abilities and character rather than on their appearance."[81]

In this context, sexual messages in media have garnered significant attention, and this academic research can inform directions in collection development. When libraries strive to increase their appeal to young people by including popular media in collections, librarians must understand the roles these resources play in young people's lives. For instance, a number of newer studies indicate sexual content proliferates across media types—so whether teens prefer magazines, the Internet, or YouTube videos doesn't matter—and it is the pervasiveness of these messages that is influential rather than simply their content.[82] These researchers also noted younger adolescents' strong interest in movies and music, which makes those media deserving of further attention. The physical and emotional changes associated with puberty make the presentation of sexuality in media particularly salient to young people's lives, and there are demonstrable effects. These associations extend to body image, alcohol consumption, and more.

Given the public health literature that promotes sexual abstinence as an important contributor to young people's preparation for adulthood, the need for balanced collection development becomes particularly important. One faction within the library community criticizes young adult literature for negative portrayals of adolescent sex—where *negative* is understood in part as involving abstinence or delaying sexual activity—and advocates incorporating an undefined positive sexuality in collections.[83] The research in communications and public health would suggest that this library-based advice on collection development misunderstands the problem: in addition to material that portrays adolescent sexuality, collections for tweens and teens should contain a broad array of attractive and engaging materials that don't focus on sexuality. Sex is a natural and normal concern during adolescence, but teens should be offered materials that encourage consideration of other issues.

Making Makerspaces

Makerspaces are making headlines. When one Oklahoma library venture, the Do Space, made the evening news recently, it high-lighted a subject that my students research to implement in their schools and that emerges during dinner conversations with friends who lead innovation at local public libraries.[84] These projects have a complex history that explains, in part, their divergent manifestations. Librarians considering whether makerspaces are in their libraries'—and teens'—future will benefit from some awareness of this context and advice that emphasizes planning and mission-oriented purpose. As community engagement becomes more central to contemporary visions of library roles, the interactions and opportunities for learning associated with makerspaces increase the appeal of these sites.

Where did the makerspaces that now seem to be everywhere begin? LIS faculty member Rebekah Willett constructs their lineage with reference to punk music and popular DIY efforts of recent vin-tage, but she and others describe a long cultural heritage behind the trend. Willett has argued, "A culture of making as a political response to mass production and industrialization can be traced back to the arts and crafts movement of the late 1800s and early 1900s."[85] Another researcher has used the phrase "evolutionary learning spaces in libraries and museums" to link the disparate entities embarked on this course, and the Institute of Museum and Library Services (IMLS) describes them as "community spaces" for "people of all ages."[86] The language libraries use to characterize makerspaces seldom highlights teens as an audience, as the sites serve multiple constituencies. This suggests why makerspaces, sometimes called hackerspaces and learning labs, in addition to the proprietary names developed by individual institutions, have so many different labels.

These origins also suggest why one common question about makerspaces is what they are. Examples of actual makerspaces and related programming may seem almost incoherent in their offerings and appeal. In one community, sewing machines factor into the equation; elsewhere, everything from malted milk balls to glitter plays a part. Other libraries promote access to pricey high-tech devices like 3-D printers, and some have taken advantage of the popularity of Little Bits electronic building blocks.[87] While one author draws on the analogy of the blind men describing an elephant to illustrate the problem of defining makerspaces, the difficulty is more complex in that the blind men had only one elephant, and we have many makerspaces.[88] The short answer, experts indicate, is that makerspaces' variety is a defining and desirable attribute.

Motivations for makerspaces are not homogeneous, ranging from the abstract to the pragmatic. Some making emerges from opposition to dominant ideologies and mass marketing, seeing handcrafted items as the antithesis of larger, depersonalizing social and political conditions. A charming explanation in a book for younger readers tells them, "Makers are people who try to improve the world around them."[89] Recognizing that contemporary tools for creativity and innovation may be costly, libraries add makerspaces so anyone can experiment with new resources. Often makerspaces provide technology and infrastructure that may be beyond individual means; consequently, some see makerspaces as an extension of libraries' enduring mission of enhancing individuals' lifelong learning.[90] Especially for younger library users, STEM and STEAM programming may be incorporated into makerspaces. Beyond offering technology and opportunities for skill-building, these centers allow individuals to meet and shape each other's projects. In other words, makerspaces support communication as well as resource access. Many proponents argue that the essential function of these centers is their potential to turn consumers into producers, a debated contention.[91] Three core concepts that define makerspaces include the material resources needed for diverse kinds of making, the possibility for open-ended or self-determined learning and creating, and opportunities for communication and sharing.[92]

These realities mean that each library needs to generate its own vision for its makerspace, congruent with its mission, goals, and community needs. One common thread that runs through media coverage of makerspaces is the relationship between what the library wants to be for its users and how resources were invested in developing its makerspace. Makerspaces may attract attention as places where users can try out prohibitively pricey technologies, but their continued utility rests on responding to actual and enduring interests. At PLA 2016, IMLS Senior Library Program Officer Tim Carrigan warned that planning makerspaces must precede purchasing materials for them. What a community wants, rather than what a library can afford, is a starting principle. Knowing the population of intended users, defining goals for the space, and having an assessment plan are also essential.[93]

Important facets of successful makerspaces include interdisciplinarity, or the integration of multiple domains or interest areas; scalability, whether to larger numbers of users or additional branches; and the creation of conditions that facilitate learning.[94] Research indicates that one benefit of makerspaces specific to younger users is the self-motivated, unevaluated nature of learning that takes place there: "No longer driven by a grade and facing fewer consequences for failure, [young people] were engaging with ideas, exploring interests in new ways."[95] These benefits accrue in part through cross-generational relationships, so youth services librarians should expect to collaborate with others to create and maintain their libraries' makerspaces.

Resources that support planning and development of makerspaces and related programming abound, and library collaboration with community partners to found makerspaces is well documented. Many libraries with makerspaces, whether located in university or public libraries, have websites to promote their missions and resources. There are books and online guides that offer model language, sample budgets, and lists of supplies needed for particular community activities and events.[96] A selection of foundational resources, as well as ones that point librarians to ongoing conversations about these initiatives, follows.

Create—Creation and Makerspaces in Libraries. www.cvl-lists.org/mailman/listinfo/create_cvl-lists.org.

> Hosted by the Colorado Virtual Library, the Create electronic mailing list started in 2014 to enable librarians to discuss makerspaces and their implementation. A related Facebook group, MakerSpaces and the Participatory Library (www.facebook.com/groups/librarymaker/), is another way for librarians to keep up with specialized news, trade testimonials, and ask questions about options they might pursue in their own makerspaces. Electronic mailing list archives are accessible only to list members.

Hatch, Mark. *The Maker Movement Manifesto: Rules for Innovation.* New York: McGraw-Hill, 2014.

> This extended vision statement does not direct librarians to adopt a particular course of action, but it does acquaint us with the way making has been popularized as a contemporary phenomenon. Along with Chris Anderson's *Makers: The New Industrial Revolution* (New York: Crown Business, 2012), Hatch's short book explores making in terms of both philosophy and commerce.

Koh, Kyungwon, and June Abbas. "Competencies for Information Professionals in Learning Labs and Makerspaces." *Journal of Education for Library & Information Science* 56, no. 2 (Spring 2015): 114–29.

> Although written for educators, this study presents guidance for those who will staff and support makerspaces in libraries. The findings, developed from interviews with individuals who work in these centers, identify skills practitioners believe most important to successfully operating makerspaces. Notably, their priorities include the "ability to learn," "to adapt to changing situations," "to collaborate," and "advocacy" over specific technical training.

Kroski, Ellyssa. "A Librarian's Guide to Makerspaces: 16 Resources." *Open Education Database,* March 12, 2013. http://oedb.org/ilibrarian/a-librarians-guide-to-makerspaces/.

> This bibliography includes, near its end, two sites that endeavor to map and collect entities creating makerspaces. Short articles that

provide energetic advocacy for the concept are central to this site. *The Atlantic* has a related overview essay, not included in Kroski's list: Deborah Fallows, "How Libraries Are Becoming Modern Maker-spaces," *The Atlantic,* March 11, 2015, www.theatlantic.com/technol ogy/archive/2016/03/everyone-is-a-maker/473286. ■

CONCLUSION

The nature of adolescents' media use has changed in recent years, with new breadth and depth of exposure generating news stories, statistics, and in-depth research. These shifts are made possible both by technology and by leisure. For all researchers and commentators that acknowledge media as a dominant factor in young people's experience of the world, their emphasis has been on its consumption, rather than creation. Although teens' invented, immersive worlds, sometimes called *paracosms,* can be found in the nineteenth-century juvenilia of authors like the Brontës, and the prototypes of zines also date to this era, teen-generated media is increasingly possible with twenty-first-century technology.[97] Fan fiction is a popular activity, with its own vocabulary and cultural norms; the first academic studies that treat this mode of authorship seriously, rather than derisively, have emerged and are expected to grow.[98] While studies of fandom have offered case studies and preliminary conclusions, much of that work has focused on online communities over the texts that teens craft and circulate online.

Advocates and scholars demonstrate teens' positive, productive, "pro-social" online behaviors, as well as what goes wrong. Most contend that the technological environment has changed, not teens themselves. Their options for entertainment are many and varied, and rather than choosing a single medium, an increasing number of teens tend to use multiple resources, sometimes simultaneously. Credible questions are being asked about media use, and doubts about the harmlessness of mediated violence or the efficacy of multitasking are being voiced by researchers with reliable data. Further, news reports about developing sites and technologies raise concerns about potential harm either to or by younger users whose as-yet-imperfect judgment may be exploited online. Teens' privacy and their ability to protect it have received renewed attention in recent years, and research indicates both teens' commitment to their rights as well as the importance of helping them understand how to limit their online sharing. Librarians need to consider these facts as they make collection, policy, and programming decisions.

It has been argued that what matters most is "how children and teens use the media and media content."[99] Particularly given young people's ability to create as well as consume media, this statement can offer direction to librarians. In addition to weeding and making acquisition decisions with awareness of the best information available on media effects, librarians can offer education sessions to help young people and their parents to make informed decisions about media use. Experts note that clearly articulated principles or norms of online conduct factor strongly in discouraging misconduct, as long as the rules are not overly stringent.[100] In supporting appropriate use of information and communication technologies (ICTs), librarians can benefit from other professionals' efforts to grapple with issues of youth development.

The media diet is a concept that could be of interest to librarians who want to encourage younger users to evaluate their media use. When I brought up this phrase in conversation with a colleague, she responded, "Oh, no! Now they're medicalizing my media!" Fear not—while some doctors have assented to the idea, the media diet is not particularly medical in nature. The fundamental idea is that media use, including time spent at the computer, should be balanced against physical activity, reading, and family interactions. This need for balance, in fact, is at the heart of what some of the most strident critics of young people's involvement with media and technology seek. Media-diet advocates also encourage parents or other caregivers to engage younger viewers in discussions of what they're seeing and to guide them in assessing ideas presented via the media. Thus, inclusive approaches to collecting media are best from a developmental standpoint. Providing tweens' and teens' parents with resources that will support their abilities to have such needed conversations with their children lets them work toward this goal.

These ideas are congruent with the notion of the library as a public good. If we serve the public and intend to use public resources wisely, pairing informed evaluation of materials with efforts to educate younger patrons about their technology use is a responsible aim. Thus, a further consideration is how the addition of technical skills and multimedia resources affects libraries. What are our motives and interests? Do we need to, in the words of one librarian, be "good at staying young" in order to serve young people effectively?[101] Or could we find other ways of connecting with young adults besides following the technological trail they leave behind them?

Numerous authorities have argued that the adults in young people's lives should strive to lead, rather than to mirror, youths' behaviors. This sort of debate has taken place in many contexts, and technology is one arena of contemporary concern. Although many experts advocate informed awareness of young people's technology use, opinion is in other respects divided. On the one hand, some say parents can connect most effectively with their children by using young people's preferred communication strategies. On the other, some experts question whether taking to the media used by teens really bridges gaps. "In modern societies, teens want to have their own cultures," said James E. Katz, a professor of communications at Rutgers University. "When the dominant culture rushes into teen domains, the teens create new domains that exclude the parental grip."[102] Then there is the middle way, as one adolescent psychiatrist has advised: learn about the technologies that teens enthusiastically adopt, rather than disapproving, but work to educate young people about safe and reasonable use.[103] This might call public librarians to look for both formal and informal avenues for promoting media and information literacy so that teens—especially those who may not be college bound—have authoritative guidance. Helping to shape young people's media use, rather than simply facilitating it, should become an element of library service. Consider a study published in *Child Development* that observed teen behavior in a chat room: teens acceded to peer pressure to engage in questionable behaviors, particularly when they believed popular individuals were sending approving messages.[104] How can we work with teens to deter media misuse? Their technology skills do not inherently allow them to form judgments about the nature of their online interactions. Enabling young people to become savvy about online safety and consumer issues as well as applauding their technical know-how is important. Research shows that teens turn to their parents for this sort of information, and that parents' information and advice are derived, for the most part, from media reports.[105] Providing educational programming about safety settings on social media and related issues, whether for teens, their parents, or both, has the potential to meet real needs. Such efforts not only respond to teens, but also offer a potential means of responding to critics who want to restrict public online access as a means of protecting young people. Good service to teens enhances their ability to acquire and evaluate information about library resources. Promoting our collections and services remains important. One of my students is fond of pointing out that local teens may be active online, but that they seldom find the library's digital resources on their own. Face-to-face conversations are her favorite way of letting them know that they can use the library online, too.

A Conversation with Jane D. Brown

How should librarians engage twenty-first-century teens' media use?

"We used to teach kids how to read *Beowulf,* now we teach them how to read *Baywatch*," Brown said. What's notable about her examples is not simply the eras in which they were produced; sexuality is a focus of much contemporary media marketed to teens, and that intersection focused Brown's research for decades. Elsewhere, she and her colleagues have observed that one question that emerges from contemporary realities concerns the number of years between sexual maturation and marriage: "Is it fair or reasonable to expect adolescents to wait so long between sexual maturity and sexual activity?" Brown and other researchers note that there is no

Jane D. Brown, the retired James L. Knight Professor of Journalism and Mass Communication and Fellow Emerita of the Carolina Population Center at the University of North Carolina–Chapel Hill.

single answer to this question in U.S. culture, but that popular media seldom suggests an affirmative answer.[106] Consequently, teens' information-literacy skills, their ability to evaluate rather than accept media messages, matter. Brown has coauthored multiple books, including *Sexual Teens, Sexual Media,*[107] and directed a five-year study of teens and media funded by the National Institute of Child Health and Human Development. Findings generated by her and her research team, which examined media use by more than three thousand young people, show two things of interest to young adult librarians: higher rates of sexual content increase teens' likelihood of having sex, and teens' descriptions of their media use indicate that their choices diverge more often than they coincide. These ideas have implications for libraries.

"It's all about selection," said Brown. "There are some good video games. There are some good magazines, and there is good music. It's a matter of being an intelligent consumer." Those who provide teens with access to media need to help young people manage their media use, she argued.

Two concepts can be applied to structuring and evaluating media use. First, Brown advocated the idea of the media diet, which encourages teens to balance the time they spend with media in relation to other activities and to limit their amount of exposure to kinds of media messages. While librarians are less likely to be involved in helping teens' structure their media use, they can make sure that information about the balancing media use and the resources that help to create diversity or balanced consumption are available. Second, there is the matter of media literacy, or the ability to critically evaluate media messages. Elsewhere, Brown has observed that mass media are often weak on the "3 C's: Commitment, Contraception, and Consequences" of sexual activity and instead direct attention to "attractive older adolescents engaging in risky sexual behavior." To convey the seriousness of these issues, not just romantic on-screen sexuality, means encouraging teens to scrutinize media messages. Together, media diet and media literacy can help mitigate the potentially harmful effects associated with sexual content. "There are ways to help your consumer understand what's beneficial to them and to critique," she said.

Brown suggested that parental and teen advisory boards could aid librarians as they strive to balance youth appeal with sound decisions. "I'm really impressed with kids' sense of this stuff. Most of them are pretty savvy," Brown said, indicating that teens are able to criticize content as inappropriate, whether due to issues of audience age or performer decorum.

Teens need material that will present sexuality differently than it is depicted in the mass media. This material, though, isn't always easy to find. "There are so few alternatives," she said. Teens need better information about safer sex and why they should wait to have sex, she said.

She acknowledged that books—*old media* to a communications researcher—are less studied as an aspect of teens' media consumption but indicated that series fiction like *Sweet Valley High* is definitely part of the picture. "Lots of girls are reading them. They're very popular," Brown said. In series fiction, more than sex is being promoted. "They're increasingly commercialized," with at least one publisher selling product placements to appear on the pages of some best-selling teen titles.

Brown indicated that at the same time that female teenagers are drawn to romance, male young adults are more inclined to sports, action, and adventure. "It's stereotypical though still true," she said. "Right from the beginning it's very gendered. What we find is especially true for television." The same patterns are true when it comes to race, Brown said. "The movies that African-American kids are going to are different than whites," she said, indicating that attracting teens to content means including media that feature characters of the same race as teens in the community. Music, however, is an area where there is more common ground. "There's more crossover in music," she said. She named BET as an example of programming that has broader appeal.

As librarians strive to reach teens, though, they shouldn't overlook young people's parents. Among the needs Brown discussed were "good books for parents to help them talk to teens." Teens need guidance, and resources for parents who are working to communicate effectively with their adolescent children would help contribute to good outcomes for young people. ■

FOR FURTHER READING

Anderson, Craig A. "Video Game Suggestions from Dr. Craig A. Anderson." June 26, 2006. www.psychology.iastate.edu/faculty/caa/VG_recommendations.html.

> This enduring, open letter offers a list of evaluative criteria for determining the appropriateness of a game for a young user, indicating key words in game descriptions that signal content with problematic aspects. He warns that ratings offered by manufacturers are insufficient and that individual products should be evaluated. Sources for games and information about them are included.

Attorney-General's Division, Australian Government. *Literature Review on the Impact of Playing Violent Video Games on Aggression.* September 2010. www.classification.gov.au/Public/Resources/Pages/Other%20Resources/Literature%20review%200n%20the%20impact%200f%20playing%20violent%20video%20games%200n%20aggression.pdf.

> This white paper article succinctly presents conclusions about video-game violence in a nontechnical way, asserting that research on the question of whether video games have harmful effects is being conducted primarily in the United States and has yet to reach definitive, long-term conclusions. Yet, we are cautioned, such research "takes place in a controversial political context of free speech disputes and school shootings" (5) and "violent crime is not easily explained by any single factor" (28). In other words, the report probes but cannot predict youth violence in U.S. culture; instead, it highlights issues such as short-term effects of violent video games, which may be more demonstrable, and the effects on individuals with other risk factors for negative outcomes. A

short history of concerns about media's influence on the young
and the violent video game in particular is included, as is an
overview of modern school shootings in this country. Analyses
of the academic literature focus on particular topics, such as
"children's game violence" (17), "vulnerable populations" (25),
and "positive effects" (37). Those who seek a sound, informed
explanation of how research on video games is carried out and
what we know as a result will find a concise summary and an in-
depth bibliography with links in this document.

Common Sense Media. www.commonsensemedia.org.

This source of reviews of movies, games, and websites operates
from a philosophy of "media sanity, not censorship." Editors and
reviewers, including teen commentators, strive to provide assessments of media appropriateness for particular ages, recognizing
that "media and entertainment profoundly impact the social,
emotional, and physical development of our nation's children."
Tips for a media diet and some other material are also available
in Spanish.

Mills, Jon L. *Privacy in the New Media Age.* Gainesville:
University of Florida Press, 2015.

Librarians who want to understand how online information sharing affects privacy will find an informed yet readable overview of
the legal and philosophical principles that govern the subject in
this book. The author believes that "Privacy and dignity matter"
(3) and elucidates how individuals' rights may be protected in
the United States and abroad. The issues discussed range from
individuals' ability to provide suppressed information through
social-media sites to how media reporting may result in misinfor-
mation. Mills raises the question of whether a pervasive lack of
privacy stifles free speech and creative thinking. A glossary, from
big data to *iReporting* to *meme,* defines relevant terms.

PBS Parents. "Children and Media": "Video Games: Teens."
www.pbs.org/parents/childrenandmedia/videogames-teens.html.

This site explains the role of video games in teens' lives, offering guidelines for ensuring that play remains positive. The tips, which discuss violence, race and gender stereotyping, product placement, and requests for personal information or face-to-face meetings, are also available in Spanish. The notes include a link for teens who are interested in careers related to video-game production.

Smith, Kathleen. *The Fangirl Life: A Guide to All the Feels and Learning How to Deal.* New York: TarcherPerigee, 2016.

By connecting young women's interest in media and the fan culture created around it with the roles and demands of real life, Smith's self-help guide urges adolescents to trade on their strengths and their passions in their transition to adulthood. Examining when interests become obsession and when they are assets, the book wants its readers to adopt the motto, "Less Anxiety, More Awesome" (xviii). Smith identifies and rejects negative stereotypes of the fangirl, explains what goes on in a fan's brain, how to "start *using* it to engage," and ways to manage the challenges inherent in relationships and work life (41, emphasis original). A brief glossary/slang guide is a bonus for librarians still sorting out contemporary fan parlance.

Stanford History Education Group. "Evaluating Information: The Cornerstone of Civic Reasoning (Executive Summary)." November 22, 2016. https://sheg.stanford.edu/upload/ V3LessonPlans/Executive%20Summary%2011.21.16.pdf.

This much-publicized report outlines the study that found many adolescents failed to distinguish between authoritative and weak information sources. Middle school, high school, and undergraduate students' abilities to identify biased material, advertisements in online content, and false news were assessed, and researchers regard the outcomes as problematic given the nature of the contemporary information environment. Researchers argue their results undermine the concept of young people as digital natives, calling for more information literacy education.

Teenangels: A Division of WiredSafety.org. www.teenangels.org/index.html.

Teens trained by law-enforcement officers promote online safety to their peers. Newer aspects of the program include a younger Tweenangels group and a special alumni group of advocates who continue to work with the program after turning eighteen. This site, which now also uses Facebook and Instagram, presents information about online safety. There are tips for teens, parents, and schools. Founded by Parry Aftab, the site has a twenty-five-year track record of providing pragmatic, informed material on subjects from cyberbullying to professional development.

Your Child: Development and Behavior Resources. "Resources on Media and Media Literacy." University of Michigan Health System. www.med.umich.edu/11ibr/yourchild/media.htm.

This collection of numerous resources offers parents and others who work closely with young people guidance on how to think about media effects. Some content is also intended for teens. Links to recent statements by the American Academy of Pediatrics and other expert groups provide quick, nontechnical explanations of research findings about cell phone use and other current concerns, like sexting and media violence. Helping young people acquire media literacy and evaluation skills is a core objective.

NOTES

1. Robert MacFarlane, *Landmarks* (London: Hamish Hamilton, 2015), 3.
2. Virginia K. Putnam, "What's New in Children's Books," address, Festival of Children's Books, Iowa City, IA, November 8, 1969.
3. Jennifer Burek Pierce, "The Reign of Children: The Role of Games and Toys in American Public Libraries, 1876–1925," *Information & Culture* 51, no. 3 (2016): 373–98.
4. "The Common Sense Consensus: Media Use by Tweens and Teens," Common Sense Media, 2015, www.commonsensemedia.org/research/the-common-sense-census-media-use-by-tweens-and-teens; Amanda Lenhart, "Teens, Social Media & Technology Overview 2015," Pew Research Center, April 9, 2015, www.pewinternet.org/files/2015/04/PI_TeensandTech_Update2015_0409151.pdf; Kirsten A. Herrick et al., "TV Watching and Computer Use in U.S. Youth Aged 12–15, 2012,"

NCHS Data Brief 157 (July 2014), www.cdc.gov/nchs/data/databriefs/ db157.pdf.

5. Adina Farrukh, Rebecca Sadwick, and John Villasenor, "Youth Internet Safety: Risks, Responses, and Research Recommendations," Center for Technology Innovation at Brookings, October 2014, www.brookings.edu/ wp-content/uploads/2016/06/Youth-Internet-Safety_v07.pdf.

6. Kaiser Family Foundation, "'Media Multi-Tasking' Changing the Amount and Nature of Young People's Media Use," news release, March 9, 2005.

7. Jeanne Rogge Steele, review, *Journalism and Mass Communication Quarterly* 82, no. 1 (Spring 2005): 199.

8. Frances E. Jensen with Amy Ellis Nutt, *The Teenage Brain: A Neuroscientist's Survival Guide to Raising Adolescents and Young Adults* (New York: Harper Collins, 2015).

9. Jay Giedd, "What Goes on in the Adolescent Brain?" video, National Institute of Mental Health, May 8, 2015, www.nimh.nih.gov/health/ topics/child-and-adolescent-mental- health/index.shtml (video no longer on website).

10. Jane D. Brown, Carolyn Tucker Halpern, and Kelly Ladin L'Engle, "Mass Media as Sexual Super Peer for Early Maturing Girls," *Journal of Adolescent Health* 36 (2005): 420–27.

11. Linda W. Braun, "Teens and Technology: An Overview of YALSA's Midwinter Institute," *Young Adult Library Services* 4, no. 3 (Spring 2006): 4.

12. For discussion of the digital native label, see Jennifer Burek Pierce, "E-books for Young Readers: A Historical Overview of Interdisciplinary Literatures," *Papers of the Bibliographic Society of Canada* 51, no. 1 (Spring 2013): 105–29.

13. "Class of 2019 List," Beloit College, 2015, www.beloit.edu/mindset/ previouslists/2019/.

14. Steven Johnson, *Everything Bad Is Good for You: How Today's Popular Culture Is Actually Making Us Smarter* (New York: Riverhead Books, 2005); Sue Ferguson, "How Computers Make Our Kids Stupid," *Maclean's,* June 6, 2005, 24–30.

15. Paula Brehm-Heeger, "Keeping Up with the New," *School Library Journal* 52, no. 3 (March 2006): 46.

16. Naomi S. Baron, *Words Onscreen: The Fate of Reading in a Digital World* (New York: Oxford University Press, 2015).

17. Marianne Martens, *Publishers, Readers, and Digital Engagement: Participatory Forums and Young Adult Publishing* (London: Palgrave Macmillan, 2016).

18. Nick Bilton, "The Allure of the Print Book," Bits Blog, *New York Times,* December 2, 2013, bits.blogs.nytimes.com/2013/12/02/the-print-book -here-to-stay-at-least-for-now/; Jim Milliot, "As E-book Sales Decline, Digital Fatigue Grows," *Publishers Weekly,* June 17, 2016, www .publishersweekly.com/pw/by-topic/digital/retailing/article/70696-as -e-book-sales-decline-digital-fatigue-grows.html.

19. Loris Vezzali et al., "The Greatest Magic of Harry Potter: Reducing Prejudice," *Journal of Applied Psychology* 45, no. 2 (February 2015): 105–21, doi:10.1111/jasp.12279.

20. Quoted in Emma Pettit, "Does Reading on Computer Screens Affect Student Learning?" *Chronicle of Higher Education,* June 22, 2016, www.chronicle.com/article/Does-Reading-on-Computer/236879?key =X-UOceseURmmRPxcYuMfbt_GUP-D6CRUbwuq9UpEiLJod11GS2py S3dWREY3cEpEUWNlVHdnNXZtdXRJSzBwdHBBMHVjZUpyX0Vr.

21. Ibid.

22. Kathleen Smith, *The Fangirl Life: A Guide to Feeling All the Feels and Learning How to Deal* (New York: TarcherPerigee, 2016), xxiii.

23. "Dopamine," *Psychology Today,* 2016, www.psychologytoday.com/ basics/dopamine.

24. Smith, *The Fangirl Life,* 39–40.

25. Ibid., 10, 11.

26. danah boyd, *It's Complicated: The Social Lives of Networked Teens* (New Haven, CT: Yale University Press, 2014), 17, www.danah.org/books/ ItsComplicated.pdf.

27. Ibid., 11.

28. Ibid., 95.

29. Sherry Turkle, "BIG IDEAS with Sherry Turkle," presentation, Public Library Association Conference, Denver, CO, April 8, 2016.

30. Bethany L. Blair and Anne C. Fletcher, "'The Only 13-Year-Old on Planet Earth Without a Cell Phone': Meanings of Cell Phones in Early Adolescents' Everyday Lives," *Journal of Adolescent Research* 16, no. 2 (2011): 156, 173, doi:10.1177/0743558410371127; Amanda Lenhart, Mary Madden, and Paul Hitlin, *Teens and Technology: Youth Are Leading the Transition to a Fully Wired and Mobile Nation* (Washington, DC: Pew Internet and American Life Project, 2005), www.pewinternet .org/files/old-media/Files/Reports/2005/PIP_Teens_Tech_July2005web .pdf.pdf.

31. Turkle, "BIG IDEAS."

32. Jensen, *The Teenage Brain,* 224.

33. Vlogbrothers, "Ending the Age of Outrage," YouTube video, July 22, 2016, www.youtube.com/watch?v=DgNSTBDEV4U.

34. Stuart Wolpert, "The Teenage Brain on Social Media," *UCLA News,* May 31, 2016, www.universityofcalifornia.edu/news/teenage-brain-social -media.

35. Lorne Manly, "Your TV Would Like a Word with You," *New York Times,* November 19, 2006, sec. 2, http://query.nytimes.com/gst/fullpage.html?res =9401EFDC173EF93AA25752C1A9609C8B63&pagewanted=all.

36. Mariana Leyton Escobar, P. A. M. Kommers, and Ardion Beldad, "Using Narratives as Tools for Channeling Participation in Online Communities," *Computers in Human Behavior* 37 (August 2014): 64–65.

37. Margaret Talbot, "The Teen Whisperer: How the Author of 'The Fault in Our Stars' Built an Ardent Army of Fans," *The New Yorker,* June 9, 2016, www.newyorker.com/magazine/2014/06/09/the-teen-whisperer.

38. Jessica McCain, Brittany Gentile, and W. Keith Campbell, "A Psychological Exploration of Engagement in Geek Culture," *PLoS ONE* 10, no. 11 (November 2015): 33/38. doi:10.137/journal.pone.0142200.

39. Ellen Wartella and Byron Reeves, "Historical Trends in Research on Children and the Media," *Journal of Communication* 35, no. 2 (1985): 118–33.

40. Dee Naquin Shafer, "Noise-Induced Hearing Loss Hits Teens," *ASHA Leader* 11, no. 5 (April 11, 2006): 1; "Samsung Urges Galaxy Note 7 Phone Exchange Urgently," *BBC,* September 10, 2016, www.bbc.com/ news/technology-37329191.

41. Christina Gregory, "Internet Addiction Disorder: Signs, Symptoms, and Treatments," *PsyCom,* www.psycom.net/iadcriteria.html; David Wallis, "Just Click No," *The New Yorker,* January 13, 1997, www.newyorker .com/magazine/1997/01/13/just-click-no; Venkat Srinivasan, "Internet Addiction: Real or Virtual Reality?" *Scientific American,* May 15, 2014, http://blogs.scientificamerican.com/mind-guest-blog/internet-addiction -real-or-virtual-reality/.

42. Jensen and Nutt, *The Teenage Brain,* 206.

43. Ellen A. Wartella and Nancy Jennings, "Children and Computers: New Technology—Old Concerns," *Children and Computer Technology* 10, no. 2 (Fall 2000): 39.

44. Farrukh, Sadwick, and Villasenor, "Youth Internet Safety," 3.

45. Patricia M. Greenfield, "Developmental Considerations for Determining Appropriate Internet Use Guidelines for Children and Adolescents," *Applied Developmental Psychology* 25, no. 6 (2004): 760.

46. Vlogbrothers, *Ending the Age of Outrage*.

47. Farrukh, Sadwick, and Villasenor, "Youth Internet Safety," 11.

48. "Multitasking: Switching Costs," APA, 2006, www.apa.org/research/action/multitask.aspx.

49. Annie Lang and Jasmin Chrzan, "Media Multitasking: Good, Bad, or Ugly?" *Communication Yearbook* 39 (2015): 101.

50. Carol J. Pardun, Kelly Ladin L'Engle, and Jane D. Brown, "Linking Exposure to Outcomes: Early Adolescents' Consumption of Sexual Content in Six Media," *Mass Communication and Society* 8, no. 2 (2005): 76.

51. Diana G. Oblinger, "Educating the Net Generation: National Learning Infrastructure Initiative," address, Educating the Net Generation, Denver, CO, October 2004, https://net.educause.edu/ir/library/pdf/pub7101.pdf.

52. Lang and Chrzan, "Media Multitasking," 125.

53. "Multi-tasking Adversely Affects Brain's Learning, UCLA Psychologists Report," *Science Daily*, July 26, 2006, www.sciencedaily.com/releases/2006/07/060726083302.htm.

54. Claudia Wallis, "The Multitasking Generation," *Time*, March 27, 2006, 51.

55. Jenny Levine, *Gaming and Libraries: The Intersection of Services* (Chicago: ALA TechSource, 2006); Sami Yenigun, "At Libraries Across America, It's Game On," National Public Radio, August, 11, 2013, www.npr.org/2013/08/11/209584333/at-libraries-across-america-its-game-on.

56. CrashCourse, "What is a Game?: Crash Course Games #1," YouTube video, April 1, 2016, www.youtube.com/watch?v=QPqR2wOs8WI.

57. Christopher Lee, "Video Games Aim to Hook Children on Better Health," *Washington Post*, October 21, 2006, www.washingtonpost.com/wp-dyn/content/article/2006/10/20/AR2006102001328.html.

58. T. Rees Shapiro, "Can Video Games Make Kids Smarter? Yale University Researchers Think So," *Washington Post*, September 15, 2016, www.washingtonpost.com/news/grade-point/wp/2016/09/15/can-video-games-make-kids-smarter-yale-university-researchers-think-so.

59. J. Peter Freire, "From Far and Wide, Video Gamers Join in a Child Charity," *New York Times*, December 27, 2006, www.nytimes.com/2006/12/27/us/27charity.html?_r=0.

60. John Gaudiosi, "Games Fight the Good Fight," *Wired*, March 27, 2006.

61. Brad King, "Educators Turn to Games for Help," *Wired*, August 2, 2003, http://archive.wired.com/gaming/gamingreviews/news/2003/08/59855.

62. "The Good Things about Video Games," *Media Smarts,* http:// mediasmarts.ca/video-games/good-things-about-video-games.

63. Catherine Delneo, "Gaming for Tech-Savvy Teens," *Young Adult Library Services* 3, no. 3 (Spring 2005): 34–38.

64. Jane McGonigal, "Gaming Can Make a Better World," TED video, February 2010, www.ted.com/talks/jane_mcgonigal_gaming_can _make_a_better_world?language=en.

65. James Paul Gee, *What Video Games Have to Teach Us about Learning and Literacy* (New York: Palgrave Macmillan, 2003), 82.

66. "Video Games: Pre-Teens," PBS Parents, www.pbs.org/parents/ childrenandmedia/videogames-preteens.html.

67. Gee initially discusses a particular game, Under Ash, when he makes these remarks but goes on to reflect on hate-group recruitment using interactive media (*What Video Games Have to Teach Us,* 155–62). He foresees an evolution of sorts, though he does not offer supporting evidence, in which violence in video games will be "replaced by conversation and other sorts of social interactions" (153).

68. "'Bully' Game Targeted in the US," *BBC News,* October 13, 2006, http:// news.bbc.co.uk/2/hi/technology/6046932.stm.

69. Edward F. Schneider, Annie Lang, Mija Shin, and Samuel D. Bradley, "Death with a Story: How Story Impacts Emotional, Motivational, and Physiological Responses to First-Person Shooter Video Games," *Human Communication Research* 30, no. 3 (July 2004): 361–75.

70. Susan Kelly, "Violent Video Game Effects Linger in Brain," *Reuters,* November 29, 2006, www.reuters.com/article/healthNews/ idUSN2822464220061129.

71. Society for Research in Child Development, "Teens' Ability to Multi-task Develops Late in Adolescence," *Science Daily,* May 18, 2005, www .sciencedaily.com/releases/2005/05/050518104401.htm.

72. Amanda Moore, "Albert Bandura," 1999, http://muskingum.edu/~psych/ psycweb/history/bandura.htm.

73. Albert Bandura, interview by Charles Harris (New York: Harper & Row, 1976).

74. Ibid.

75. Richard I. Evans, *Albert Bandura: The Man and His Ideas—A Dialogue* (New York: Praeger, 1989).

76. Renee Hobbs et al., "How Adolescent Girls Interpret Weight-Loss Advertising," *Health Education Research* 21, no. 5 (2006): 719–30; "Call for Children's Food Ad Curbs," *BBC News,* November 3, 2006, http://

news.bbc.co.uk/2/hi/health/6110378,stm; Susannah R. Stern, "Messages from Teens on the Big Screen: Smoking, Drinking, and Drug Use in Teen-Centered Films," *Journal of Health Communication* 10 (2005): 331–46; James D. Sargent et al., "Alcohol Use in Motion Pictures and Its Relation with Early-Onset Teen Drinking," *Journal of Studies on Alcohol* 67, no. 1 (January 2006): 54–65.

77. Pardun, L'Engle, and Brown, "Linking Exposure to Outcomes," 84.

78. Steven C. Martino et al., "Exposure to Degrading versus Nondegrading Music Lyrics and Sexual Behavior among Youth," *Pediatrics* 118, no. 2 (August 2006): e430–41.

79. RAND Corporation, "RAND Study Finds Adolescents Who Listen to a Great Deal of Music with Degrading Sexual Lyrics Have Sex Sooner," news release, August 7, 2006, www.rand.org/news/press/2006/08/07.html.

80. Rob Potter, "Gender Differences in Response to Sexual Lyrics," *The Audio Prof,* May 12, 2006, http://theaudioprof.blogspot.com/2006/05/gender-differences-in-response-to.html.

81. Jane D. Brown, "Media Literacy Has Potential to Improve Adolescents' Health," *Journal of Adolescent Health* 39 (2006): 459–60; Task Force on the Sexualization of Girls, *Report of the APA Task Force on the Sexualization of Girls* (Washington, DC: American Psychological Association, 2007), 7, www.apa.org/pi/women/programs/girls/report-full.pdf.

82. Pardun, L'Engle, and Brown, "Linking Exposure to Outcomes," 88; *Report of the APA Task Force on the Sexualization of Girls,* Executive Summary.

83. Amanda M. MacGregor, "Let's (Not) Get It On: Girls and Sex in Young Adult Literature," *VOYA* 26, no. 6 (February 2004): 464–68.

84. Bill Kelly, "In Omaha, a Library with No Books Brings Technology to All," *All Tech Considered,* National Public Radio, May 31, 2016, www.npr.org/sections/alltechconsidered/2016/05/31/477819498/in-omaha-a-library-with-no-books-brings-technology-to-all.

85. Rebekah Willett, "Making, Makers, and Makerspaces: A Discourse Analysis of Professional Journal Articles and Blog Posts about Makerspaces in Public Libraries," *Library Quarterly* 86, no. 3 (July 2016): 313–29.

86. Kyungwon Koh and June Abbas, "Competencies for Information Professionals in Learning Labs and Makerspaces," *Journal for Education for Library & Information Science* 56, no. 2 (Spring 2015): 114–29; *Learning Labs in Libraries and Museums,* 4.

87. Cindy R. Wall and Lynn M. Pawloski, *The Maker Cookbook: Recipes for Children's and Tween Library Programs* (Santa Barbara, CA: Libraries Unlimited, 2014); Matthew Hamilton and Dara Hanke Schmidt, *Make It Here: Inciting Creativity and Innovation in Your Library* (Santa Barbara, CA: Libraries Unlimited, 2015).

88. John J. Burke, *Makerspaces: A Practical Guide for Librarians (Lanham,* MD: Rowman & Littlefield, 2014), 2.

89. Samantha Roslund and Emily Puckett Rodgers, *Makerspaces* (Ann Arbor, MI: Cherry Lake, 2013), 6.

90. Katrina Schwartz, "What Colleges Can Gain by Adding Makerspaces to Their Libraries," *Mind/Shift*, February 5, 2016, ww2.kqed.org/ mindshift/2016/02/05/what-colleges-can-gain-by-adding-makerspaces -to-its-libraries.

91. Willett, "Making, Makers, and Makerspaces," 316.

92. These principles are derived from several documents, including *Learning Labs in Libraries and Museums: Transformative Spaces for Teens* (Washington, DC: Association of Science-Technology Centers/ Urban Libraries Council, 2014), www.imls.gov/assets/1/AssetManager/ LearningLabsReport.pdf.

93. Tim Carrigan, "The Intentional Makerspace: A New Framework for Making and Learning in Libraries," presentation, Public Library Association Conference, Denver, CO, April 7, 2016.

94. Ibid.

95. *Learning Labs in Libraries and Museums*, 7.

96. Hamilton and Schmidt, *Make It Here*; Leslie Preddy, *School Library Makerspaces* (Santa Barbara, CA: Libraries Unlimited, 2014); Michelle Hlubinka et al., *Makerspace Playbook*, school edition (Spring 2013), http://makered.org/wp-content/uploads/2014/09/Makerspace-Playbook -Feb-2013.pdf.

97. Paul Armstrong, "How Historical Is Reading? What Literary Studies Can Learn from Neuroscience (and Vice Versa)," plenary talk, Reception Study Society, IPFW, Fort Wayne, IN, September 26, 2015; D. M. Smith, "Print Networks and Youth Information Culture: Young People, Amateur Publishing, and Juvenile Periodicals, 1876–1890," Ph.D. diss., University of Illinois, Urbana-Champaign, in progress.

98. In contrast with Jenkins's earlier *Textual Poachers*, new titles include Karen Hellekson and Kristina Busse, eds., *The Fan Fiction Studies Reader* (Iowa City: University of Iowa Press, 2014).

99. Steele, review, 199.

100. Farrukh, Sadwick, and Villasenor, "Youth Internet Safety," 4.

101. Brehm-Heeger, "Keeping Up with the New," 46.

102. Ken Belson, "A Parent's Guide to Teenspeak by Text Message," *New York Times*, November 26, 2006, www.nytimes.com/2006/11/26/weekinreview/26belson.html?_r=0.

103. "Tips for Parents," *Time*, March 27, 2006, 50.

104. "The Price of Popularity," *Denver Post*, July 24, 2004.

105. Farrukh, Sadwick, and Villasenor, "Youth Internet Safety," 7.

106. Jane D. Brown, Jeanne R. Steele, and Kim Walsh-Childers, *Sexual Teens, Sexual Media: Investigating Media's Influence on Adolescent Sexuality* (Mahwah, NJ: L. Erlbaum, 2002), 3–4.

107. Jane D. Brown, *Sexual Teens, Sexual Media* (New York: Routledge, 2001).

Six

Working with Teens in Libraries

Afterexamining what cognate fields know about subjects that concern us—whether teens themselves or media created by and for them—a further consideration is the relationship between what we know and what we do as librarians. What is the relationship between knowledge and practice, between studying youth culture and working in the community? How, given what we know, do we think about our profession?

Once, it was possible to believe that serving teens was simple. One of the first treatises about library service to teens, *The Fair Garden and the Swarm of Beasts,* was published in the late 1960s. In it, Margaret Edwards described library work with adolescents "as simple as ABC," where *A* is "sympathetic understanding of all adolescents," *B* refers to "firsthand knowledge of all the books that interest them," and *C* equals "mastery of the technique of getting these books into the hands of adolescents."[1] This attempt to demystify

159

young adult services was a noble and perhaps strategic one, but only a few years later, YA librarians across the country augmented her narrative with their heartfelt ideas about "fresh approaches to services (and literature) related to sex, drugs, and rock 'n' roll."[2] Librarians regarded what they were doing as a mirror for the changes wrought in the Age of Aquarius that "called for consideration of the whole teen, as well as materials and services that spoke to larger social issues."

Edwards, whose work in libraries came about after she was fired from her job as a high school teacher after questioning her principal's authority, was part of a colloquy among YA librarians about how to work within institutional culture while reaching out to teens who felt at odds with societal norms. Cindy Welch has characterized Edwards as a "noted YA advocate/activist librarian," and Edwards recognized that efforts to provide contemporary, engaged services and resources were sometimes controversial.[3] Some aspects of Edwards's model endure, not least because of the way she welcomed change. She decried the way public libraries found themselves "stuck fast in yesterday" while the world around them developed new bases for their interactions with young people. She urged librarians to be aware that

> lawyers are beginning to say that they must cease to rely so heavily on decisions made in the past for this is a new age with new problems. High schools are seeking to interest more young people in finishing their educations and colleges are reexamining their philosophy and curricula to gain the confidence of young people. Ministers and priests often join with youth to protest injustice, and the Catholic mass has been set to the music of young people.[4]

Edwards's expressions may sound slightly quaint to readers accustomed to twenty-first-century memes and Twitter feeds, but the topics she identified resonated with her peers in the 1970s and are of renewed concern in the twenty-first century.

A recent conversation with one library director about the traits she looked for in the process of hiring new librarians revealed both traditional and innovative expectations. She listed things like people skills, teaching experience, and some knowledge of youth materials. Technology skills, plus familiarity with youth-specific contextual knowledge, whether preliteracy skills or brain development, are also desirable. Most important, however, was "a passion to continue learning." For YA librarians, this can mean everything from mastering a new technology to improving one's understanding of that core constituency.

This library director posed an interesting question to characterize the service philosophy she wanted to see staff adopt: "Where do we say *no* when we want to say *yes?*" This well-phrased question asks us to evaluate long-standing practices, the way we've always done things, and consider whether they might be barriers to serving our communities. If rules and policies about overdue fines and losses, for example, reduce teens' access to library materials and create barriers between them and us, do our practices actually serve our aims? One of the things I have found inspiring, as our school's graduates fill me in on their professional lives, is their efforts to recognize and rethink the way rules intended to structure teens' library use impede it. They describe creating computer-room-specific cards to allow teens with fines, or those who would have problems getting a library card, access. They're less interested in creating an idealized sense of the teen years in their libraries' spaces than in learning what teens, particularly the underserved, truly need.

Other fields pursue new courses of action based on new knowledge, too. In the wake of recent research on the adolescent brain, for example, lawyers have raised questions about when it is appropriate to charge teens as adults, successfully challenging a number of laws that had normalized this practice. Schools, including colleges and universities, continue to assess instructional practices in light of changing technology and other contemporary developments; everything from the relevance of general education requirements to the structure of the semester is being reassessed at institutions from Georgetown University to two-year colleges. Libraries have found themselves in the spotlight when protests in their communities flare, notably in Ferguson, Missouri.[5] While much media attention focuses on a stridently secular popular culture, in some communities religion continues to inform the values and the priorities that teens encounter in their daily lives.

Where Edwards saw other institutions as models for change that libraries should emulate, today, other organizations represent potential partners for libraries. Edwards's fundamentals may seem, on their face, bibliocentric, and newly fledged librarians will find job ads that emphasize the need to work with others over knowledge of materials. From cooperating with professionals in different library departments to school outreach, sample ads suggest that collaboration is as important as collection development.[6] Some libraries describe this community engagement trend as "turning outward," a service philosophy that sees librarians supporting activities well beyond library walls.[7] It is becoming the new normal in public libraries.

In addition to standard partners, like area schools, YA librarians will want to consider who else might be invested in teens' growth and community engagement. Uncovering those potential partners may be well understood where you work, or it may require considerable effort. There are multiple ways librarians can develop familiarity with potential community partners. When I last worked as a youth services librarian, the county sponsored a meet-up of all municipal department staff, with short, introductory talks to identify key areas of activity, followed by time to chat informally. At PLA 2016, Denver-area librarians described a lengthy and involved environmental scan that identified organizations and offices with related goals.[8] A former social worker told me that state agencies may also have lists of entities involved in improving outcomes for teens. Looking for information on how the increasingly important topic of partnerships has already been approached in your community may be a logical starting point for endeavors of this sort.

These kinds of community connections add a significant component to the work of the teen librarian, who also needs some grasp of the diverse types of materials for teens, including resources that could support young people's creativity. Once, a student confessed to me her deep desire to work with young people, to help them learn and use nonfiction tools, along with her fear that her secret antipathy for the YA novel would be her undoing. There are, of course, any number of antidotes to this difficulty, from readers' advisory tools to reader-recommendation sites. Professional literature, electronic discussion lists, and proliferating awards identify new and worthy material for us. My students know well my response to recommending popular fiction, borrowed from a conversation with a wine merchant. As we walked the aisles of the wine shop, we passed a display for a wine that I'd tried at a restaurant and found overly and unpleasantly sweet. Surprised by the attention being drawn to what I could only think of as a not very worthy wine, I asked if he'd tried it. "I don't have to," he said, "It sells itself." This, to me, is a sensible response to best-sellers that don't intersect with one's personal reading preferences. You need to know they exist, to be able to help a reader who wants to locate them but can't remember a title or a genre or who doesn't realize that there's likely a hold list for the latest hit. You don't need to pore over every page, taking in nuances of style, theme, and character. One librarian friend recommends reading as much as a chapter for a sense of the work, time permitting.

The environment in which we function differs dramatically from the days when Edwards broke new ground with her efforts to make teens welcome in the library. Instead of combing adult collections and an emerging teen-oriented publishing market for the relatively few books suited to the adolescent reader, there is a dynamic array of resources for adolescents, including opportunities to connect with well-known authors and materials they themselves produce and circulate. Even a truly voracious reader would be little likely to acquaint herself with everything created for adolescents in the twenty-first century, although less than a hundred years ago Edwards found it quite reasonable to expect a young adult librarian to read everything on the department's shelves. The changing and proliferating information environment is one signal of the need for new approaches to working with young people in libraries.

Understanding materials available for young people, along with the increasing knowledge generated about the young people we strive to serve, means there is much for librarians to assess as we try to maintain reasonable fluency with the themes and vocabulary of youth culture. It is clear that we must understand more than popular culture as we develop the professional activities that help young people read, think, and increase their literacy skills. New information about developmental issues and the implications of ICT use suggests we ought not simply rush in where youth desire to tread. The value of our own professional education ought to involve the ability to make assessments grounded in information from researchers who belong to other disciplines as well as testimonials about young people's new-found passions.

Further evaluating the work we do with teens would enhance the development of contemporary services and collections for teens. Noting that much more research is needed on this aspect of library services to young adults is not a startlingly original contention, but the truth of it endures. One avenue, beyond the long and complex aim of growing our own research community, involves understanding empirical, scholarly conclusions about the effects of the media we collect. In addition to speaking to teens and to one another, as we do via electronic discussion lists and blogs, we need to account for the voices of others who work in the content area and have begun to establish core knowledge. Then, beyond a snapshot of what occurred—how many teens attended a program or how many items circulated—the types of knowledge and behaviors that emerge afterward would help demonstrate the value of library services to the community. Some library directors refer to this as a shift to documenting outcomes, rather than outputs, and their interest in the difference stems from their investment in the broader effects of what we do. One way to pursue information about how people's lives can change because of what libraries offer would be through the theories proposed by cognate fields, which seldom accept attitude as a predictor of future actions.

This book's survey of the contemporary research landscape for cues about how to understand young adulthood does not offer, to borrow one of Edwards's metaphors, "provender for beasts." Its focus is on how to think, on reframing our view of young people rather than offering straightforward ideas about how to encourage them to use our libraries. In this, it is both informed and speculative, seeking conclusions from emerging research mostly untested in our libraries.

What it does suggest, though, is that some assumptions we've used to ground decisions aren't fully borne out by empirical research. With the best of intentions and the backing of what once was valid theory, advocates for young adults argued that teens are independent and fully capable individuals. The indications emerging from inter-disciplinary research in recent years, though, suggest that teens benefit from supported decision making. Teens are still in the process of gaining important cognitive, social, and emotional maturity. Welcoming parents and other professionals positioned to aid young people is a possible avenue into collaborative relationships, congruent with the YALSA mission. In other words, truly empowering teens might mean something somewhat different than we've assumed in recent years. It is to our advantage, and to teens' benefit as well, to draw on the growing body of knowledge about adolescence and media as we reflect on our ideals for professional service.

In this, we do not have to reject the alphabet that Edwards relied on. We should, however, use it to construct new vocabularies and ways of talking about the needs of our teen patrons. We need not work alone to determine what might be appropriate in light of the emerging ideas about adolescent development and the effects of media; we should find partners, others who want to connect with teens in the twenty-first century. Years ago, Edwards called on us to invite young adults into the library wholeheartedly; having done so, we ourselves now must venture outside it.

NOTES

1. Margaret Edwards, *The Fair Garden and the Swarm of Beasts* (New York: Hawthorn Books, 1969), 16.
2. Cindy C. Welch, "Dare to Disturb the Universe: Pushing YA Books and Library Services—with a Mimeograph Machine," *ALAN Review* 37, no. 2 (Winter 2010): 59–64, doi:10.21061/alan.v37i2.a.9.
3. Ibid.
4. Edwards, *The Fair Garden*, 116.

5. "Q&A: What Happened in Ferguson?" *New York Times,* August 10, 2015, www.nytimes.com/interactive/2014/08/13/us/ferguson-missouri -town-under-siege-after-police-shooting.html?.

6. WebJunction Connecticut, Young Adult Librarian, Town of Anywhere, *OCLC Web Junction,* 2012, www.webjunction.org/documents/ webjunction/Young_Adult_Librarian_Job_Descriptions.html.

7. "Extraordinarily Engaged: How Three Libraries Are Transforming Their Communities," Public Library Association Conference Program, Denver, CO, April 5–9, 2016, 40.

8. Kellie Cannon et al., "Teen Asset Mapping: A Community Development Approach to Teen Services Expansion," Public Library Association Conference, Denver, CO, April 5–9, 2016. The presenters have shared the project details and supporting materials in a Google Drive folder at http:// tinyurl.com/DPL-teen-mapping.

Leading and Managing
Youth Services

Youth services librarians are managers and leaders, roles acknowledged by the inclusion of
administrative and management skills in the diverse
competencies that YALSA and ALSC set for practitioners. Regardless of whether librarians are division
or department heads, as professionals they allocate
their time to ensure that core tasks are completed, see
that funding to support programming and collection
development is used responsibly, and more. Even
librarians who don't supervise staff must cooperate
with peers and professionals in cognate positions in
the community as well as host programs with multiple participants. They communicate with the public
through blogs and may be interviewed by local reporters. These varied responsibilities involve aspects of work
conventionally associated with library management.

While each library has its own practices and norms
for scheduling, training, and other routine operational

activities, multiple fields contribute to our understanding of leadership and management. Optimal strategies for internal and external communication, for facilitating staff engagement, for time management, and other aspects of organizational culture should be informed by relevant research. Much writing about these issues is designed for application, and it is oriented to the development of best professional practices. In addition to guiding our work, these ideas may also aid us when we are asked to formulate or review library policy.

Leadership and Organizational Culture

While for a time it was common to decry *management* in favor of *leadership,* most experts agree that these terms refer to two different, necessary skill sets. Individuals at all levels of responsibility in libraries are expected to demonstrate leadership skills, as they factor strongly in the overall work environment and translate into improvements in patrons' experience of the library. The articles below are classic and contemporary perspectives on how leadership can and does result in a positive environment for staff and library users alike.

Heskett, James. "Why Isn't Servant Leadership More Prevalent?" *Forbes,* May 1, 2013. www.forbes.com/sites/hbsworkingknowledge/2013/05/01/why-isnt-servant-leadership-more-prevalent.
> This brief article defines *servant leadership* as a particular kind of accountability and involvement, looking at its antecedents as well as its more recent practice. The positive results of this management style are highlighted, and a bibliography for fuller exploration of the subject concludes the piece.

Lisker, Peter. "The Ties That Bind: Creating Great Customer Service." *Public Libraries* (July/August 2000): 190–92.
> Libraries need customer service plans as a means of ensuring their objective of serving the public. Lisker presents reasons to articulate meaningful strategies for encouraging satisfying interactions between staff and patrons, as well as intangibles that factor in staff performance.

Schwartz, Tony, and Christine Porath. "Why You Hate Work."
New York Times, Sunday Review (June 1, 2014): SR1.

Schwartz and Porath discuss the deficits of prevailing organizational culture and managerial strategies for helping employees feel engaged. They note that meeting employees' needs in four critical areas enables demonstrably stronger work performance. By increasing staff autonomy and decreasing a 24/7 culture, employee satisfaction and retention also result.

Sowards, Steven W. "Observations of a First-Year Middle
Manager: Thirteen Tips That Can Save You." *C&RL News*
(July/August 1999): 523–25, 541.

A brief examination of the department manager's role in libraries, this article advocates respect, realism, and recognizing optimal strategies for accomplishing goals. It identifies a few further resources for librarians who seek more guidance on how to manage library staff.

Todaro, Julie. "The Truth Is Out There: Reasonable Expectation
of Adult Behavior." *Library Administration & Management* 13,
no. 1 (Winter 1999): 15–17.

This article describes personnel problems as the "single most compelling" issue faced by library managers; in this, it echoes themes that emerged in discussion of draft standards for accrediting library education programs during the ALISE 2014 meeting. Todaro presents language and objectives for managing difficult situations.

Urban Libraries Council. "Leadership Brief: Library Leaders
Owning Leadership." Summer 2012. www.urbanlibraries.org/
filebin/pdfs/Leadership_Brief_Final_061112.pdf.

This brief best-practices guide references and highlights the contemporary leadership literature in the course of identifying and defining five assets and skills library leaders should cultivate. Dynamic contemporary settings are the institutional context for the guidance provided here.

Communication

Communication takes place in mediated and non-mediated environments. Librarians exchange ideas face-to-face, in print, and through any number of digital means. The importance of these interactions is undisputed. Even before the twenty-first century, anecdotes about the results of inadvertent miscommunication, particularly via e-mail and other online media, had become pervasive, while few stories about positive communication practices have achieved the status of common knowledge. The articles below are ones whose authors engage the sometimes difficult aspects of communication in contemporary work life.

Cross, Rob, and Laurence Prusak. "The People Who Make Organizations Go—or Stop." *Harvard Business Review* (June 2002): 105–11.
> Informal communication can support organizational goals. Four different, typically undesignated, roles reflect the presence of social networks that transmit information within an organization. Analysis of these communication patterns can lead to improved information sharing. Librarians in smaller settings may consider this classic study of contemporary communication practices in large organizations as a framework for interorganizational communication.

Hedges, Kristi. "Harvard Business Review Webinar: Five Essential Communications Skills to Catapult Your Career." *Harvard Business Review* (September 5, 2014). http://blogs.hbr.org/2014/09/5-essential-communications-skills-to-catapult-your-career/.
> A webinar focusing on workplace communication skills, this hour-long talk gives attention to effective presentations, communicating with staff about new initiatives, and communication in distributed environments.

Urban Libraries Council. "Leadership Brief: Libraries Igniting Learning." Summer 2013. www.urbanlibraries.org/filebin/pdfs/L_Brief_IV_Learning_Full_Rep.pdf.
> This short document offers guidance on why and how libraries are poised to help with community goals like improving learning

outcomes. Ways to communicate the library's role as a supporter of lifelong learning to different audiences are a core theme. Examples of library messages about its support for learning are included.

Welch, Cindy. "Keep Your Friends Close and Your Staff Members Closer: Internal Advocacy for Youth Services." *Tennessee Library Association* 60 (2010). www.cci.utk.edu/ bibio/keep-your-friends-close-and-your-staff-members-closer -internal-advocacy-youth-services.

    In a practice-oriented discussion of interdepartmental communication, Welch offers ten suggestions for improving communication with staff outside youth services. This is a vital and concise overview of how to work well within the organization that gives attention to the need for education and renewal.

Time and Resource Management

Drucker, Peter F. "Managing Oneself." *Harvard Business Review* (January 2005): 2–11.

    This excerpt from a full-length book focuses on self-awareness and how understanding one's personal strengths and weaknesses translates into a more effective organization. Although at times appearing to give credence to now-dated ideas about learning styles, Drucker argues that one's time and skills are among the resources a manager must use to achieve organizational aims.

Flatow, Ira. "The Myth of Multitasking." *Talk of the Nation,* radio broadcast transcript, National Public Radio, May 10, 2013. www.npr.org/2013/05/10/182861382/the-myth-of -multitasking.

    The concept of multitasking is a popular one, so much so that the skill even appears in job ads. Increasingly, though, cognitive scientists and psychologists cast doubt on its effectiveness. This interview provides an accessible discussion of the fundamental problems created by multitasking as a work strategy.

LaRue, James. "Assessing the Assessment Center." *Wilson Library Bulletin* 64, no. 3 (November 1989): 18–21. www.jlarue.com/assessment_center.html.

LaRue describes conventional approaches to job interviews and outlines an alternative strategy. While labor-intensive and costly, the model represents an important perspective on hiring practices.

Rice University/Ceridian Corporation. "What Does It Take to Plan and Run a Productive Meeting?" *Youth in Action Bulletin* (September 1999). www.ncjrs.gov/html/ojjdp/yb9909-1/mtg-2.html.

This document calls attention to specific practices that are likely to result in an effective and useful meeting. It explains how to proceed when multiple people meet for a specific purpose.

Snyder, Herbert W., and Elisabeth Davenport. *Costing and Pricing in the Digital Age: A Practical Guide for Information Services*. Library Association Publishing, 1997.

Librarians who must evaluate options for paying for goods and services will find guidance through an array of case studies and commentaries on managing budgets and resources. The intricacies of paying for online materials and the economics of leasing rather than owning equipment are among the scenarios discussed.

Varnet, Harvey, and Martha Rice Sanders. "Asking Better Questions." *C&RL News* (June 2005): 461–65.

Varnet and Sanders argue that the success of library assessment projects is driven by the framing questions. They offer examples of productive questions that libraries can answer with readily discernable metrics.

Emergencies

Sendaula, Stephanie. "Active Shooter Policies in Libraries: ALA Annual 2016." *Library Journal* (July 5, 2016). http://lj.libraryjournal.com/2016/07/shows-events/ala/active-shooter-policies-in-libraries-ala-annual.

This article offers an overview of dos and don'ts from a 2016 ALA conference session on armed attacks. The article includes links to pages providing further information and discusses responding to a shooting as an element of a disaster plan.

Volunteers

Welch, Cindy. "Teen Volunteers to the Rescue!" In *How to Thrive as a Solo Librarian,* edited by Carol Smallwood and Melissa J. Clapp, 69–82. Lanham, MD: Scarecrow Press, 2012.
Combining philosophy and pragmatics, this very readable chapter guides librarians in the successful recruiting, training, and maintenance of a teen volunteer program. Attention to the concept of scaffolding, or structured learning experiences and evaluation, is central to this practical explanation of how to ensure successful working relationships with young people.

Law, Policy, and Ethics

Most often, youth services librarians are municipal employees; that is, the libraries in which they work are divisions of city or county governments. As such, we are governed by the laws and practices that have been adopted by these entities. Independent library districts differ in this respect, but as tax-funded entities, they still hold positions of public trust. While librarians aren't lawyers, we must be aware of the legal and ethical principles that govern our work. Laws affect our interactions with patrons as well as staff members, as do professional norms governing patron privacy and related matters. It is important to remember that a hierarchy of law exists in the United States, so that federal laws, like the First Amendment to the U.S. Constitution that creates our right to freedom of speech, have implications for decisions made at lower levels of legal authority; such laws trump professional association policies in terms of the authority they carry and the responsibilities they create.

Further, young people, who for the most part, are under the age of eighteen, have a different legal status than adults. While we strive to respect and to nurture the needs of young patrons, as minors, further considerations affect our work with them.

The federal statutes and national organization policy statements listed below are ones whose broad precepts youth services librarians, particularly those in management roles, should be familiar with. Library Leadership & Management, a division of ALA, or LL&M, provides a guide to helping staff understand the privacy rights created by these and other legal documents: www.ala.org/llama/sites/ala.org .llama/files/content/publications/orienting_and_educat.pdf.

Americans with Disabilities Act
www.ada.gov/ada_intro.htm

Children's Internet Protection Act
www.fcc.gov/guides/childrens-internet-protection-act

Equal Employment Opportunity Commission
www.eeoc.gov/eeoc

Family and Medical Leave Act
www.dol.gov/whd/fmla/

PATRIOT Act
www.justice.gov/archive/ll/highlights.htm

ALA's Privacy and Confidentiality site
www.ala.org/Template.cfm?Section=ifissues
&Template=/ContentManagement/ContentDisplay
.cfm&ContentID =25304

ALA's Library Bill of Rights
www.ala.org/advocacy/intfreedom/librarybill

ALA's Freedom to Read Statement
www.ala.org/advocacy/intfreedom/statementspols/
freedomreadstatement

If your library is constructing or reviewing its local policy statements, a number of online resources can guide your work. As a youth services librarian, you are likely to be asked to consider matters like unattended children, especially in the event that young teens don't have a ride home at closing; appropriate uses of library computers, including rules for any video games the library intends to purchase; and challenges to materials, which disproportionately accrue to items collected for younger users. The following sites document specific library policies, often with reference to optimal procedures such as the regular review of documents that guide library practice and the creation of new policy as technology and culture change.

- Iowa City Public Library's comprehensive policy documents are at www.icpl.org/policies/.

- The fifty-nine-page Mississippi School Library Media Guide is located via this Mississippi Department of Education page; although some elements are state-specific, it is a well-researched document providing model statements on many aspects of school library and media service: www.mde.k12.ms.us/docs/curriculum-and -instructions-library/mississippi-school-library-guide -2014-new.pdf?sfvrsn=2.

- The New Mexico State Library has collected library policies from libraries around the nation to guide local practice: www.nmstatelibrary.org/services-for-nm -libraries/programs-services/librarians-toolkit/samples -recommended-policies-for-public-libraries.

- WebJunction links to policies on a range of library subjects, including e-reader access and other current issues: www.webjunction.org/explore-topics/policies -procedures.html.

- Wisconsin's Department of Public Instruction provides multiple resources germane to youth services work in libraries, including policy statements, best practices, and more: http://dpi.wi.gov/pld/yss.

Essential Reading for Young Adult Librarians

Bernier, Anthony et al., comp. "Two Hundred Years of Young Adult Library Services History." *Voice of Youth Advocates* 28, no. 2 (June 2005): 106–11. http://voyamagazine.com/2010/03/30/chronology.

Identifying and documenting pivotal moments in library services for teens, this chronology was first published in *VOYA* in 2005 before moving to an online format. Key figures and publications, ALA/YALSA history, and cultural context are combined in this overview of how young adult services have developed in U.S. libraries.

Booth, Heather, and Karen Jensen, eds. *The Whole Library Handbook: Teen Services.* Chicago: ALA Editions, 2014.

This book's strengths are its pragmatic advice regarding the day-to-day work of teen services:

planning, programming, managing collections, and promoting inclusive services.

Curry, Ann. "If I Ask, Will They Answer: Evaluating Public Library Reference Service to Gay and Lesbian Youth." *RUSQ* 45, 2 (Winter 2005): 65–75. http://pacificreference.pbworks .com/f/If+I+Ask,+Will+They+Answer.pdf.

Curry examines how teens perceive librarians' responses to reference questions about LGBTQ issues. The evaluation of service signals ways that public librarians may need to enhance their approachability and nonjudgmental responses to queries.

Gaiman, Neil. "Why Our Future Depends on Libraries, Reading, and Daydreaming: The Reading Agency Lecture, 2013." In *The View from the Cheap Seats: Selected Nonfiction,* 13–26. New York: William Morrow, for HarperCollins, 2016.

Gaiman, in his inimitable way, probes the question of how we know which books are written for young people. Editorial decisions about marketing his award-winning *Graveyard Book* and other titles to younger readers factor in his discussion of how books shape us and our world.

Holt, Glen E. "Fitting Library Services into the Lives of the Poor." *The Bottom Line* 19, no. 4 (2006): 179–86.

Holt raises questions about what it really means to serve underserved community members whose financial and living conditions may create inherent barriers to library use. He differentiates between passive declarations that the library and its services are available to all, regardless of socioeconomic status, and policies and outreach that will meet disadvantaged community members where they are. Equal parts inspiration and action-oriented advice, this essay is essential reading for every public services librarian.

Learning Labs in Libraries and Museums: Transformative Spaces for Teens. Washington, DC: Association of Science-Technology Centers Urban Libraries Council, October 2014.

This report offers one of the few in-depth overviews of how makerspaces became a bridge between STEM programming and youth services. By encompassing broad ideas about mentoring and goal-directed ones about education and business development, the report signals the interests that lead libraries to invest in makerspaces. Potential model sites, outcomes, and other empirical conclusions are featured.

A Mighty Girl. www.amightygirl.com.
When women's history highlights are shared online, A Mighty Girl is often the source of information. With bibliographies of related resources and more information, the site can readily support active and passive readers' advisory.

Myers, Christopher. "Orlando." *Horn Book Magazine* 92, no. 5 (September/October 2016): 12–15. www.hbook.com/2016/06/opinion/orlando/.
This impassioned essay explores dance clubs like the site of the 2016 Orlando shootings as places where identity develops and community is created. Making sense of the tragedy, Myers argues, depends "more than answers," on "stories that recognize the fullness of humanity" (13, 15). With his acknowledgment of the annual ALA conference in proximity to Orlando and the mass shooting, Myers sees librarians as essential to a more peaceable and united future.

Pierce, Jennifer Burek. "Why Girls Go Wrong: Advising Female Teen Readers in the Early Twentieth Century." *Library Quarterly* 77.3 (July 2007): 311–26.
The history of youth services is sometimes framed as a narrow and repressive past that contemporary librarians must reject to meet young people's needs. This article demonstrates that librarians have a long history of genuine interest in teens and creative, connected services reflecting interdisciplinary understandings of what it means to be a young person in U.S. society.

Riordan, Rick. "Rick's Reading Recommendations." http://rickriordan.com/resource/ricks-reading-recommendations/.
As a self-confessed reluctant reader and parent of readers of a similar bent, Riordan identifies appealing titles for those who struggle to find an engaging story. In an interview with Audible

following the first of the *Kane Chronicles*, Riordan noted that reading recommendations are not a one-size-fits-all proposition, so his lists offer options, not absolutes. He updates his recommendations in his News section too. His responses to other authors are generous and eclectic, as demonstrated by a July 10, 2016, post that recommends a video on science fiction written by women and books from Octavia Butler's *Parable of the Sower* to Justin Cronin's *City of Mirrors* and *Beyond Magenta: Transgender Teens Speak Out*. Librarians may also be interested in the Guys Read initiative at guysread.com, where Jon Scieszka leads efforts to identify books, including pop-up books and audiobooks, that young men across the age spectrum will find appealing.

Scales, Pat R. *Books Under Fire: A Hit List of Banned and Challenged Children's Books*. Chicago: ALA Editions, 2015.

Books Under Fire updates and replaces ALA's earlier *Hit List* series, which identify books frequently targeted by censors. These quick guides offer plot synopses, key complaints against each title, and related details of prominent or particularly notable challenges to library materials. Awards and other information that will help librarians respond to censorship, or even difficult conversations with patrons, are included.

Stevenson, Noelle, Grace Ellis, Shannon Waters, and Brooke A. Allen. *Lumberjanes* series. Los Angeles, CA: Boom! Studios, 2014–2016.

I just discovered these fantastic, punning, girl-power graphic novels, and you shouldn't leave to chance whether or not you read them.

Strauss, Valerie. "Is Listening to a Book 'Cheating?'" *Washington Post*, July 31, 2016. www.washingtonpost.com/ news/answer-sheet/wp/2016/07/31/is-listening-to-a-book-a -cheating/?postshare=7131470138146151&tid=ss_fb. Originally published via Daniel Willingham's blog: www.daniel

willingham.com/daniel-willingham-science-and-education-blog/
is-listening-to-an-audio-book-cheating.

Cognitive science professor Daniel Willingham's expert opinion is that audiobooks provide many of the same benefits of print-based reading. Willingham discusses one model of reading, described as the "simple view" involving decoding, or comprehending print, and language processing, the broader cognitive act of making sense of language. There is no single, simple answer, as audiobook use varies with age, "types of texts," and purpose. His clever metaphor endorses audiobooks: "Listening to an audiobook might be considered cheating if the act of decoding were the point; audio books allow you to seem to have decoded without doing so. But if appreciating the language and the story is the point, it's not. Comparing audio books to cheating is like meeting a friend at Disneyland and saying: 'You took a bus here? I drove myself, you big cheater.'"

"Transition—Adolescents to Adulthood." *Council on Contemporary Families*. https://contemporaryfamilies.org/topics/transition-adolescents/.

Offering highlights and links to research on current topics, this site makes unfolding, interdisciplinary research accessible. Aspects of school, family life, and even economics effects are considered here, and many other subjects, including LGBTQ families, are a focus elsewhere on this CFC site.

Urban Institute. "Adolescents and Youth." www.urban.org/research-area/adolescents-and-youth.

The Urban Institute's ranging research on contemporary issues intersects with the concerns of teens in numerous ways. The Adolescents and Youth portal, which describes the Urban Institute's interest in "the challenges facing youth as they transition to adulthood" and directs readers to studies and reports, engages topics such as dropping out of high school, digital badges, and more. A blog reports on here-and-now topics like the concentration of Pokémon Go stops in white neighborhoods.

Vlogbrothers. "Why the Word 'Millennial' Makes Me Cringe."
YouTube video. January 29, 2016. www.youtube.com/
watch?v=bSGqz_SE1uM.
> John Green identifies and discounts prevailing stereotypes about young people in the twenty-first century.

Welch, Cindy C. "Dare to Disturb the Universe: Pushing YA Books and Library Services—with a Mimeograph Machine."
The ALAN Review 37, no. 2 (Winter 2010): 59–64.
> It's easy to think of library history in terms of the late nineteenth-century origins of the profession, and Welch's essay on young adult librarianship in the 1960s and 1970s offer a corrective in the form of critical developments in more recent years. Her work describes how librarians used available, pre-Internet technologies to create a national network of individuals committed to teen advocacy. Mimeographed newsletters and oral histories create a vivid portrayal of a vital time in the development of young adult services. Today's emerging librarians will recognize the passion and the perspective in their words.

"Youth Matters" column. *American Libraries* magazine.
> Developed in 2007 to respond to the growing number of librarians involved in youth services, this column gives attention to current issues and topics of interest.

Index